Urban Myths: 210 Poems

John Tranter has published twenty collections of verse and is the editor, with Philip Mead, of the *Penguin Book of Modern Australian Poetry*, the standard text in its field. He has lived at various times in Melbourne, Singapore, Brisbane, and London. He now lives in Sydney where he is a company director and the editor of the free Internet magazine *Jacket* at jacketmagazine.com

Other books by John Tranter

Poetry and Fiction
 Parallax
 Red Movie
 The Blast Area
 The Alphabet Murders
 Crying in Early Infancy: 100 Sonnets
 Dazed in the Ladies Lounge
 Selected Poems (1982)
 Under Berlin
 The Floor of Heaven
 At The Florida
 Gasoline Kisses
 Different Hands (fiction)
 Late Night Radio
 Blackout
 Ultra
 Heart Print
 The Floor of Heaven
 Borrowed Voices
 Studio Moon
 Trio

Anthologies and compilations
 The New Australian Poetry
 The Tin Wash Dish (poetry)
 The Penguin Book of Modern Australian Poetry (co-editor)
 Martin Johnston: Selected Poems and Prose

Notes to accompany John Tranter's poems can be found at
johntranter.com

Urban Myths: 210 Poems

John Tranter

SALT

CAMBRIDGE

PUBLISHED BY SALT PUBLISHING
PO Box 937, Great Wilbraham. Cambridge PDO CB1 5JX United Kingdom
PO Box 202, Applecross, Western Australia 6153

© John Tranter, 2006

First published 2006

Printed and bound in the United Kingdom by Lightning Source

Typeset in Swift 9.5/13

ISBN-13: 978 1 84471 252 6 paperback
ISBN-10: 1 84471 252 4 paperback

TB

Contents

From *Borrowed Voices* 2002

After Hölderlin

When I was a young man, a drink
often rescued me from the factory floor
or the office routine. I dreamed
in the mottled shade in many a beer garden
among a kindness of bees and breezes,
my lunch hour lengthening.

As the flowers plucked and set in the little bottle
on the table still seem to hanker for the sun,
nodding in the slightest draft, so I
longed for a library loose with rare volumes
or a movie theatre's satisfying gloom
where a little moon followed the usherette
up and down the blue carpeted stairs.

You characters caught up in your emotions
on the screen, how I wish you could know
how much I loved you; how I longed
to comfort the distraught heroine
or share a beer with the lonely hero.

I knew your anxieties, trapped
in a story that wouldn't let you live;
I felt for you when you were thrown from the car
again and again; when the pilot
thought he was lost and alone,
I was speaking the language of the stars
above his tiny plane,

murmuring in the sleepy garden, growing up
among the complicated stories.
These dreams were my teachers
and I learned the language of love
among the light and shadow
in the arms of the gods.

From *Parallax* 1970

The Moment of Waking

She remarks how the style of a whole age
disappears into your gaze, at the moment
of waking. How sad you are
with your red shirt, your features
reminiscent of marble, your fabulous
boy-girl face like a sheet of mist
floating above a lake.

Someone hands me a ticket,
in Berlin a hunchback
is printing something hideous;
my passport is bruised with dark blue
and lilac inks. Morning again,
another room batters me awake—
you will be haunting the mirror like silver—

now the nights punish me with dreams
of a harbour in Italy—you are there
hung in the sky on broken wings
as you always have been, dancing,
preparing to wound me with your
distant and terrible eyes.

The City, the Tree

1

The city allows the trees a little space
at the edges of the road that angles
somewhere out to the airport
and the open sky, which is also permitted
to burn its flaring shadow on the tar.

The trees wave and clatter,
warning us of something, the city
is always busy, and when at rest
is better left alone.

2

This is the response the tree has
to the city: the film of lime
the skein of birds-feet, morning
polishing the blue windows of the yacht club
where the tree reflects itself
in a thousand images of green.

The Visit

The children stoned us, the bony girl
fell down bleeding at the mouth
frightened for her camera's sake;
later we drank beer in the courtyard
of the smelly afternoon, talking of Rijeka.

At the city's edge we found a monument
split down the middle; the sunlight,
preparing for the moment of anguish
laid out a stroke of warning on the rock.

The shabby soldiers wheeled in the street
or loomed out of helicopters, fondling guns.
Their movements are elegant and simple;
a sundial for a face, and memories
of Birmingham and postcards of the sea.

At the final wharf the children were playing
and we gave money to the blind man at the gate.

Kabul

From the broken, moving window
you see them alone in the desert afternoon
mad and burnt in a chorus of camels
walking somewhere invisible.

They have buried a city in the mountain.
A river like a soggy drain, they wash their feet
thinking of Tashkent gleaming out of Russia
across a plain of ice, the clack of a rifle bolt,
four thousand British corpses in the pass.
They dream their legacy of light
whatever the season.

Rescue

The mountain broods on its own nightmare
in a blanket of clodded snow.
Michael slithers over the hump
on long whispering feet, pearl blue at the collar,
zipped and tangy; the bright air
razoring the cross of blood and ice.
Here is the flag for the ascension.
The lady smiles, toasting her legs in a blanket,
plotting the brisk chopper-blades of evening
and the melody of dark—she thinks the mountain
fingers up a tasty dream—he angles over
to loosen the strap, the moon
bloated yellow, waits behind the ridge.

Whitey

At dawn, there was a knocking about
on the cold verandah, Whitey had come home
with both barrels hot to the touch.
The smell of cordite etched into his face.
Well, what a trip, what a journey;
the day's work done.

The next morning the view
from the verandah was an empty bite—
a stretch of cold grass led down to the trees.
Whitey was walking about down there
in the gloom of the trees like a pale
memory. Very intent
on a casual moving about,
both barrels cold as ice.
Well, what a morning, someone in the house
was making coffee.

The Plane

The plane drones low over Idaho,
a thundering shadow on the wheat.
The captain is thinking of a dust-cloud
disappearing out to sea.

The heavy wings tilt, a silo
looms abruptly. The cloud
falters on the horizon of his mind.
Taped to the cockpit wall is a photograph,
a piece of Sunday afternoon,
a lawn, a bright dress, flowers.
Soon they will be flying over the mountains
in a halo of ice. The cloud
hangs about, behind the imaginary trees.

The Non-commercial Traveller

We found him down by the creek
crouched into the mud bank.
'Well, I'm lost . . . took the wrong road . . .' as though
this foreign river was somewhere near town,
or the roadway up on the mountain.
He was locked up in a really neat
suit. His face shone
behind the white shirt. 'Say, phew . . .' Very odd,
David had to laugh. Nobody said much.

I noticed how easily we stood
on the bare earth. His shoes
 seemed to puncture the ground.
'Well, I'm sorry,' he said, 'for all this.
I'm a commercial traveller. Lost my bag,
samples, whatever . . . don't bother looking.
Please go away.'
                We looked back from the ridge,
at the dull green foliage and the gleam of water.
There he goes, said David, into the river
laughing or crying, at this distance
difficult to tell.

Mary Jane

I am the diver with the metal lung
pumped full of gas. One, down; two,
pull the pin. The shellburst of memory.

When I open the happy book
the snapshots flick at my eyes,
I become as bland and vicious
as an empty window. Then you are
mobile, coloured, supper to the greedy heart.
Watch how I lock my head
and gulp the key. Light the taper.
See the armchair full of time. Night. The city
hesitant on the balcony. Listen. The dream
crawling through the garden.

I wake into tomorrow full of rain,
unprepared, guessing the taste of flesh
ash-grey and sweaty on the bone.

Machine

He lay in the sheets, almost
a corpse, throttled by awkward tubes.
'They are like cold fingers,' he said.
Something pumped a fluid. The flowers
brightly blue. 'I shall never walk, of course.'
Moving his face up into the room,
'It is easy,' he said, 'everything
moves.'

Paint

'a poem should be as comprehensible as life itself...'

The scholar finds time to teach
what should be taught.
Someone is grateful for the load.
Meanwhile his younger brother paints,
caught in dangerous red, breaks loose
runs into the street in black leather.

The scholar, being old
would think of 'rouge' and 'noir'
a tricky synthesis . . .

the younger brother grovels in a bath of red.

From *Red Movie and other poems* 1972

Balance

The traveller slouches at the table
handling the glass of pale sour liquid.
In the dim corner someone plays a mandolin
and the heat wavers at the door.

He can see the bus crawling away
into the desert. Having arrived nowhere, he finds
a portion of despair like a gun
settling into a comfortable balance in the hand.

Bestiary

She haunts the bar in a loose, meandering fashion
imprinting glasses with lipstick and not caring.
Her mouth is bright and shoddy, having tasted
a 'little too much'. There are two paths of approach:

the youth hangs about in a grey cloud
of relative eagerness, biting the hand that admonishes.
Middle age flaunts the yellow stripe
of wisdom. The barman sees three animals
coiling in the imaginary grave.

Ward Five

A wrinkled print of myself
stumbles across the grass.
He has lost his grip
and has fallen off the world.

The trees creak with malevolence
as he passes, face averted,
the shadow of a grimace flickering
across his lips.

What is eased forth as a sigh of despair
comes out a strangled grunt;
what is meant a gentle gesture
to the sunlight and the flying air
becomes a nervous claw shaking at his mouth

poor child
'princely nature of our elder brother'
drowning in the polar night

'. . . may you not be long on the way!'

On the Track of the Attainable

The ambitious minister from the smaller nation
outside the borders of history
through a lack of the will to be
makes up for flesh deficiency with another woman.
He has a bitter smell like a sick uncle that nobody wants
having good reason to drink failure.

Another night plunges into darkness
and symbols of alcohol and flame.
He rushes across the city
from one flesh garret to another
gathering evidence of bones under the face
and articulated structures of pain.
He cries that he is ravished with the threat of death.
'My bones crack and tremble under the dirt!
My teeth mangling the worm!' Nightmare
made incarnate in every foul breath!

The larger nation affords an expansive smile
and wears golden ambassadors like a blessing
fingering out to Rio, Guadalcanal, Korea
fond in the delusion of money and the teeth of life.

Red Movie

*That which can be studied is the pattern of
processes which characterise the interaction of
personalities in particular recurrent situations or fields
which 'include' the observer.*
        — HARRY S. SULLIVAN, in *Tensions That Cause War*

1. *The New Field of Knowledge*

when the new alphabet soup of the earth
is raised into a flag, the inevitable wind appears
with its own 'sister to breath'.
the streamers appeared, he grew forward,
as though a new field of knowledge
drew breath, promised itself

a blue field will always invade you.
here, you can become a little more
becoming: the streaming sister,
enveloped in a flag of brutality, draws a ration
of sense, bleeds rationality.

a willow's image follows me into the dark
a delicate cowboy, so blue, his dawn
sky
is
too.
        ∽

we breathe like fish in this
glass-tinted gloom, the music room.
plugged in. headphones. out there

the grass deepens from a washed-out yellow
to a solemn green.

we drift across the lawn.

standing at the entrance
to a cold landscape filled with rain
firing into the trees, the gun
bucking against your heart.

London. 5 a.m. summer.
the sodden corpse of a monkey
floating on the oiled canal.

evening, the woman crouches in the flare
reflected from the new ocean.

thoughts of silver oppress the lake
        :such light

opening a way through.
        I'm thinking

2. *Extract from the Ice Diary*

he apologised for the delay
owing to illness
one accurate acknowledgment of the place of dirt
one brief flirtation with 'owing to illness'
a couple
of reparations, cancelling the attainment

I will always want something like you

     ∼

a man settles onto the earth
pursuing a small rodent in a dreamy light
hoping for 'escape'

a man repairs his only dream with blunt fingers
unused to despair's tesselation, how he
unravels the structure

     ∼

the creek bleeds with a little blue

we see the pieces of the dream

carefully arranged, but lacking a certain touch
the pressure, the requisite alchemy

so the cloud, the rain
complete the picture
almost to perfection the creek

a dreaming flag billows out
a wet stripe of green

     ∼

an experiment which succeeds, he said,
wiping the breath from his face
is no longer an experiment, but has become
a demonstration of the obvious.

this said, as he struck out at the images
gathered on the mountain
to drench him with the gust of life.

～

hunger developed a bitter attitude.
we were more deprived
as the night grew, finally filling the sky.

one thing I prophesy: light will spread
from the other rim of cloud.

～

a desert, this appalling gaze
allow it to pervade the skin
that encapsulates a bitter taste of blue
proffer the blade
in the hope of an eloquent movement

forgive her face
for what it cannot conceal
offer something without hope
of a receptive 'attitude'

I will always invade you

prepared to ascend the stair

loosen up, become aggressive
let her warm you up
if that becomes a problem

départ! départ!

'ma faim'

~

the poem will allow you to move. a girl is burning
in her underwear. leaving this continuum in rags
shattered desert . . . he can allow me to travel
from this insight:

stopped the track. if this trick
I will allow you to depart

'if it's all you want'; how piteous, such a mistake
brings back a river of what you can least afford
in your present extremity: God bless you

in your present grasp
of an unidentified illusion

as if resisting a new stripe of colours
a whole street . . . I'm thinking. . .
in a new suit of hands
                              . . . as though fallen
from a shelf of ice, newly frightened,
he prepared the scent of mint for the roadway

a new cloud appeared. a helicopter chopped its way
through the blue
his blades
are
too

~

the small man polished up the regiment:
they stood about on dawn parade.
the sun drifted through the mist behind the trees.

across the gravel road, in the bushes
were some bona fide travellers, also
skulking. something else happened. to the poem

~

an experiment which has failed is no longer
an experiment, it is, he smiled,
nothing more promising than a failure.

~

listen to me: you're enjoying nothing
seen from this crisp angle

listen to me: I have been travelling for some time
aware of the necessity for choice: move!
if you wish to unravel the sources of your own sorrow
if you wish to divert the river of absolution
if you are desperate for a chance
to break up

choose the song most suited
to your movements, to your fatal
and impossible beauty

summer's tattered flag your winding sheet
fate's tackle and gear
drops you by the neck

whatever song you bring
to the country of hope

3. *The Death Circus*

the death circus moves in.
all you're worth is in it
the man with the plastic face
opens up his graves for you to see

the lady with the soft legs
opens up in the night
all the moon
long, the bitter light
chews at our faces. you will not like
the happy flame circus in the roaring dark

we were taking a ride
way out south, somewhere you have never been
into a country of cold beauty
the salamander circus
followed like a hungry dog

4. *The Failure of Sentiment and the Evasion of Love*

morning hunches like a gathering of men
in damp overcoats, waiting for something to happen

shudders into light: the death transfusion breaks
some news: confusion of tongues

flesh in the oral cavity! slips
across the lip as the big dude
breaks down: sack of slack meat on the flash divan

broke up and cried like a baby.
you'll help me pick up the pieces,
won't you, my prince of light.
won't you, won't you,

~

she disheartens into a dirty bed
huddling a knoll of pleasure to herself.

the light goes peachy. something
trundles out of the forest. morning
edges a little nearer.

he investigates the hospital where her mind
will have to be repaired. nothing he could do
would warm the ravenous flesh,
none of his movements
blunt the starved edge.

he thinks he is ready to go somewhere
but the gasoline reeks out of the tank
blood runs from the fingers like red ink
from a leaking pen.

now the girl stands in the concrete yard.
her eyes go white, reflecting
the sky she has come to love,
that has so little of the human in it.

her look turns back against her with a jealousy
beyond repair.

~

he said: I could have moved, but
only to wound. unlock
the gentle embrace. like water.

much later, the return:
his sight broken,
drowned, his face
soft as water.

whenever he altered his appearance she would cry
he became less concerned

how do you know I have loved you?
why do you return? is it my flesh? you want?
to touch? why do you inflict yourself?
how am I guilty? who is it,
in the shadow of the forest?

'ce n'est rien: j'y suis, j'y suis toujours . . .'

~

there is something about flesh
which defeats me. or hair
flowing into light. you
you know these movements,
you with your 'big smile'.
come here, bring me the liquid
left overnight to breed
'big dreams'. I hear the blind man's tap
tapping at the pane. he brings his own music.

as your body moves in the glass, your hands
wound me. thus. moving. such
music, music, music; the mind
preparing the re-entry program
controls the tiny movements of air.

you say this music
has the power to maim;
I know such a gesturing of flesh wavers
on the border of its own reflection. movement.
Love. the wall of noise.

～

I am leaving in the morning, says the
young husband of a few days. yes.
break my heart if that's what you want. that's not
what I want. bring me the coffee.
cold again. why I love you

look at you, you're crying, shit you're a nasty
coward, to hurt me. like this.
look at your eye, blowing up,
filled with water.

～

your breast is very round, if such
geometry were possible. juice,
of a sort, is promised. he says
let me alone, he says *bitch teeth*

later they are alone
with an animal for company they call
cat, or the night
trembles into neon, or the morning
hurts over the sleeping city, crying
breast, breast,

~

he throws away the glass
prepared to be damaged

he makes machinery of his arms
that were accustomed to giving

a black hood protects him
from Nothing

a shout from the street
breaks red into his vision:
he desires something like himself

~

shaving, the razor warps in the glass
and slides beneath a rusty green film.
behind his shoulder, a window
choked with white. she
slouches at the end of the hall, an angry girl
gaping at the bright windy hill and the sun
washing the street. *youth breaking into age*
corrupts reflections of itself

when I sleep lately it's a black kingdom
pulls me under like a tide

Khan coming out of Mongolia—
changes from the outside,
Egyptian traits . . .

the question that inevitably comes.

5. *The Knowledge of Our Buried Life*

the dreadful sailor fills the dark
with his strange descant, building

sepulchres of ruin in the past.
to make him go, the dumb tongue

wallows in the mouth. in the courtyard
rain flares on the cobbles

the fountain flails the rocky lip
and will not cease. he reaches an exhausted sleep

late at night, and dreaming of Asia.
darkness resumes the tables, and the sailor

filled with night and the ocean, departed
as one leaves a sleeping port

at dawn, the water gleaming from below
and the harbour silent.

    ~

improbable alterations overtake the coolest nightmare:
though each is a clear flag of the dreamer
it turns up the soil in his own field like a stranger.

the struggle of objects against their fate
is not cancelled: the field fluctuates as the act of seeing
imprints the world with the reflections of a colder dream.

    ~

the fog grows from the harbour's leaden mirror
discovered by a pale dawn

correcting the village's advance
into day. *aube*, he said, *aubade*

at a faint distance someone cried a noun
as some presence awoke from the steep hill

and moved down to the sea which was speaking
in the voice of gulls

aubade

aubade

      ~

I would like you to unwrap the mood
most suited to your present grasp
as though you could control the desire
of your own wasteful preparation

I think we are in winter again
if you are ready
we can begin

From *The Blast Area* 1974

The Guadalcanal Motel

They hold no holidays at the Guadalcanal Motel;
the Sergeant stumps about the dusty yard
trying out his new leg and the President weeps
in his spider-web study, while the peons
run chattering off the rocks and drown themselves
in the grey Pacific. They make no mourning,
keeping part of their trivial sorrow in reserve
for the day when it will be needed again,
for the night when the blue troops splash ashore
and rake the sandhills into patchwork ratshit,
bringing the Guadalcanal Motel into the arms
of the New Republic amid a litter of spent shells.
They haunt the American conscience like a rotten nightmare
in a flicker of old movie clips: 'Platoon Five!
Take the hill!' And the ambulance drivers
weep and slash the air with glass slivers
from a shattered windscreen. They take no leave,
beating the stubborn earth with blunt clubs
in a travesty of agriculture, and ripping up
whatever foliage they might encounter, which is not much,
green being a surreal and worthless luxury
in the Motel trenches. Each morning they salute the statues

of the ancient king who sold them into slavery
and the franchise king who brought them
money, poverty and Coca-Cola.

Poem Ending with a Line by Rimbaud

He: It is easier to like the soldier
when he laughs and shoots a foaming dog
rather than a man, or child, and easier then
to hold the hand grenade. No plane comes
down faster when the jets are shot
than the law of gravity allows. Let the radar
plot, let the men drink poisoned lemonade.
It is better to allow the tide
to bring the fish in as they will,
or in that shoal as that shoal moves
like a flock of leaves across the hill,
across the traffic and the school of windscreens
damp with love. Leave the office,
leash the dog that nibbles at his bone,
bring all your country longings to an end.
Prepare your face to be an imprint of the scene—
the clock, the limping man, the cash machine.
Wax the ski. Compress the snow.

She: *Et mon bureau?*

Compromise

Certain vehicles are produced for luxury. Some
are not. The engineer removes his overcoat
and steps into the spartan frame. Steel surrounds him,
fittingly. He moves the vehicle at great speed
along the motorway. The girl in the skimpy mink
climbs into the leather seat and rushes about
in a frenzy of comfort. She would like more speed!
Other vehicles have the aim of brutal power.
The staff of the engineer are all regretful,
attempting to steer a middle course.
They come together in a new design:
staff, engineer, the girl who gets around.
They move about the highways in a game of elegance
dreaming of metal, markets, power, contradictions.

The people of the countryside also move about,
strapped to the spartan frame of compromise.

From *The Alphabet Murders* 1976

The Alphabet Murders

1

After all we have left behind
this complex of thought begins
a new movement into musical form, much as
logic turns into mathematics and automatics
turn into moonlit driveways—'form at the edge
of hearing', almost, like a locomotive whistle
late at night becomes a linguaphone and then
jumps into bright focus like a lunatic
aware that hunger concentrates the mind
and means lunch straight away—we mean
poems right away and no fooling.
So I write to you 'from a distant country'

2

Before this complex thought begins attacking
what we have left behind—riddles, packaging—
itself must generate enough good luck for the whole voyage.
After trunkfuls of bullshit dumped overboard
and the page alive with noise and verb geometry
I'm ready and lunch jumps into sight and we are off
like a rocket, zooming through the lecture hall where
history becomes a kind of thick paralysis and breaks
down into spasms and morality and all we can remember
through the fog of confusion is how we thrilled
and brought back memories of Captain Marvel
wriggling on a pin, or in the lens' meniscus
held to the niggling eye.
No more literature. The dream is done.
But take precautions: oil the gun, unsheath the pen
and grease the new appointment if you will
for we are not all as easy as the one who hides

in the shadow of the sun and clicks the shutter
at the briefest flick of eyelid or the wettest smile.
I have been keeping a dopey vigil in the tower
to show I'm not mad and making notes
as to the behaviour of the 'lesser sex'.

3

Cool it, with all the friends of scholarship to hand
there should be little fright, so take it easy
riding through the night. Now
the craftsman turns away from domesticity
with its pattern of submission, cliché and reproach
and retires to a house in the countryside.
It is English, autumn, smoky and reposed,
badgers wander across the great lawns in the evening
and the peaceful rhythms of another, better life
claim him piece by piece. He sits musing
in front of an open fire, sketchbook at hand,
as the tapestry weaves its message in the shadow chambers
at the rear of that condominium we call his brain.
Is it inspiration? Is it luck? Is it duty,
that sour globe of perspiration on the nerve?
He grows, the nimble fingers fly, the pattern
reels an arabesque across the paper. Five years later,
with a hearty laugh, he is gone from the country;
then abroad—there are rumours of a sighting
in Dogubayazit, in northern Turkey,
and after that, nothing. And the tapestry?
It is now a joke, a dirty parable
that kids laugh about in school, it is a lesson
that everybody hears and no one understands,
it now hangs in Texas in a renovated castle
and entertains the visitors immensely,

and like some long and boring poem by Matthew Arnold
in which the bloodstained burning battlements of Art
rise up in Hauteur from the sodden Turf
it puffs itself up and explodes all over the onlookers.
It is a bladder bloated with its own conceit, and yet,
rhymed or free, retarded or advanced,
as the poetry of life spirals upward in the smoke
from this great and almost mythical work of art
the skills of horticulture carry on, a million clerks
fill out a questionnaire, the grand pursuit of excellence
convicts itself of nothing, and is praised.
So in his Tartar yurt, his books abandoned,
he becomes the amateur and once again
begins that climb through craft to frightful insight
while all I can do (me! me!) is eat page after
page of this 'plain speaking' in a rhetoric
dazed with ambiguity. You might say that
no career is adequate to my melancholy, as it's
true that no whip is suitable
for my desire, but that's all bullshit
and a different kind of western movie makes it clear.

4

Drifting through the gritty, adolescent Western novel
we find a boundless buried geography jutting up
just underneath the reader's attention-span.
The annual outing of the Literature Society was held
on the foothills near the Epic Volcano, an area
noted for its inhospitable terrain and noxious gas . . .
Suddenly the mountainside shudders, belches
and blows up with a lewd cracking noise,
showering the explorers with hard poetry turds.
These little fragments of lyric

fall like tiny brains from the sky
fertilising the lakes and great rivers.
The heavy unpeopled fields that lie
sodden under the mass of tangled verbiage,
the banks of snow that scud back and forth, these
outward symbols of the mind's recalcitrance
plunge us into thinking again and again
and we drive deep into trouble with our queer friends
in the hope of meeting something vast and possible.
What's it like in there? Do we need confidence?
Is a casual knack enough? And we fade away.

5

Ecstasy is the Master of Lunacy and calls the tune
you said, and when he sweated on the bed you retold
some of the ancient craftsman's memories:
'The boats broke against the breakers, and though
we came to the coast in the season of storms
we had wounded warriors, and the sail torn. At dark-fall
rocks dropped down from the cliff, one breaking
the decking, though without great damage.
Behind the border, burning beacons,
thus we were worried where to wend on our going.
We wanted green water beyond the reef.
These are the feared: water, fire, rock and foe.'
All that babble gone down the chute of years
and now a tale to stop up little frolic.
A gaggle of story-tellers followed into folly.
How do we sort it out? The gilded lie,
the tempting truth about a pretty boy
who gambled with a mighty tongue and lost his wits?
('as one hog lives on what another shits . . .')
'The wild men were hidden half out of water

behind the highest rocks of the reef, and with the longboat
low laden, many made the deck. There was much killing,'
tells the chronicle, though without regret.
What would the Norsemen say? being
busy at their butchery, a kind of trade,
and having neither need nor knowledge of remorse.

6

Fate is a variety of religious experience which is
always asking its own questions, for it is only
a reductive problem, or the essential gesture
behind every question that a little boy might
store away for the future when he stands up
in the midst of the great Lesson and testifies
'I doubt that there's a problem left that hasn't
crawled beneath a book, protecting its value
in the manner of a whimpering aristocrat
in the year of the "Red Tide", or can we only bleat
being so deprived of images by greedy Futurists
(of how the Duke of Money sucked a spanner
and called it infinite delight, surpassing beauty . . .)
or whether radical gestures
of the more political kind are fit
too neatly to the hawker's palm and politician's arse
and are thus rubbed between the two as if
the only love we were permitted by the Sonnet
was onanistic and deprived, or is it
hope to crawl out of the hole that language
laid us in?' He is not a child, his face
is rainy by now and the class dissolved, he has
forged a destiny from the language and his teachers
must decide to punish him and lead him on
into those areas of doubt and sickness where he grows

suddenly beyond their narrow estimates and breaks
their shackles and the test record and
breaks into a valiant and vacant freedom.

7

Get lost: it might work in a stable society but don't
try it here sonny; we're on the lookout for mistakes
you'll be the first to go we generate
information in the bowels of the earth
and call it 'Happy Holiday, my Good Consumer!'—
the heart abandoned and the tongue forked,
the language binary and don't complain—
we eat 'journalists' for breakfast and 'authors'
for dessert, and if you're clever you're a digit.
You will be pleased to learn we have philosophy:
'No line of syllables can satisfy the Sonnet's
greed for flesh horizons. One dawn repeats
another morning as though metal mocked, becoming
several typewriters at once, and, uh, the
identity code to generate multiple patterns
of rhyme in the cavities of the computer's fear.
Mmmm . . . music, like a river full of dead
vegetables, and that smell like ice on the vein,
and that paradise of shops. You can make it.'
We came back to that liner
who drew the line at the unreachable horizon.

8

How are we locked into the forme that is
history in the making? At night, when
the mothy lamp flickers and shadows crawl

across the lawn, we dream of a perfect history
and pray that our children will be included
in the small reward that trickles out of action.
Is it too late to stare at ourselves cruelly as we must
if we really want that freedom, or are the little fears
that grow out of human contact and avoidance
and the knowledge of all those terrible old stories
too much even for the willing soul? How do our
acts and gestures, falling through the years,
shore up the silly things we do, the way we
argue and cause pain and hurt our friends with lies,
and make us grand? Grander than we deserve, we think,
and then sob and break down and no guiding hand . . .
for we have chosen to be free and quite abandoned
and, like a salesman driving to a crucial meeting
in a new convertible, hoping that the number
in his pocket will lead not into labyrinths of choice
but rather to the much-deserved promotion he has
grown accustomed to through books and television
and who imagines dialling and the sweaty phone and
the avalanche that middle age and masturbation brings . . .
like that small and smelly man we lose hope
just at the city limits and give away the game.
For history is a kind of city, dusty in the quarter
where rats and garbage bury our best illusions
so that something old is seen as something broken
and ignored, and any fresh idea or politician's trick
glints over the rim of the new developments
where orphans, children of ourselves and kin
to those we now imagine, play in a cold
and futile light that sweeps in from the sea
reminding us of those even further reaches
where shapeless things toss on a dark wind.

9

I find myself alone in a room full of stupid poems
I have a searching pain in the neck
I am going to move to Bermuda where
I believe life is innocent and in the pink
I find the pain congratulating itself
I have some of the questions and a bank account
I know how to kill a rabbit and a lobster differently
I know each lives and dies according to its kind
I think constantly on those who blundered badly
I don't think we've met I'm sorry was that your
I've had enough of 'literature' God damn
I'm caught in the throes of a merciless poem
I'm having a ball I said look out
I don't have any answers isn't that what they say?
I'd certainly love to is that all right?
I am always about to make a serious study of the word
I, and it's always just too late goodbye Mister President
I'm sorry we never met I could have healed your wounds
I think occasionally on those who were truly great
I hope you like the puzzle that
I sent—goodbye Superman goodbye

10

Justice is a kind of rhyme,
though metaphysical and like an epigram.
He who lays his life along the line
will bite the poison pill, and in the throng
the patriot will be anathema.
An afterthought: 'I wish you well.
Goodbye to all pretension. Keep it clean.
Remember Left is Right, and Right is Wrong.

Wipe the gun and polish the machine
and Politics will sing you to your rest.
Keep notes, and nothing more, and make it neat.
The simple honest tone is always best.'
The epigram: 'The shoes will shape the feet.'
Much later, when the season had grown oppressive
with an alien heat, I found myself adrift in the city.
The puzzle glittered in the ruins of the street
beneath a building like a broken tooth.

11

Karl Marx is a comic novelist, almost—
but when we read *Das Kapital* between the jokes we find
there is a theory of religion, then one of philosophy,
a quick adventure and a sordid tale of justice, and soon
a kind of parable emerges like a shadow on a screen:
man is born, grows up and dies. But if this is all he says
we would be cheated, and the authority of the work
is proof of something more than entertainment.
It is like a factory which, on weekdays,
choked and smoking in a frenzy of industry
yet holds prospect of a new revival of the workers,
and which on the weekend sinks into a profound silence
that embodies not only the concept of the modern
forty-hour week, but also the executive's retreat
from that which, though stained and horrible,
provides him with a pretty secretary, a young boy,
a lunch account, and fears of bloody revolution.
(Don't cry at the end of that novel, it's pointless
unless you cry glycerine which is sly and tricky
and all the kids here will love you for it
you witty bastard and envy your 'attack'
or your nerve and pat you on the back and then

leave you to your own devices.)
And think of this: each Russian movie masterpiece
bears his stamp, more than an individual approach,
which is like—uh—like a buried emblem
of the work itself, a tiny mirror for the plot—
or maybe narrative—and in this frame
the image, drift and meaning of the total work
act out their small and wistful life.
Outside this interlocking blazon, a lifestyle
called 'the film' takes place happily
night after night millions of times
as wasteful and expensive as a Russian dictionary
and more misleading than the tracks it leaves
entering and leaving your life,
and what is that? Snow, politics, the cruel city,
that goodly pedagogic food you ate—
all right, I'm moving, through a dense topography
keeping an eye on how the colourful natives
act out a plausible way of seeing it
for our benefit as we hike away,
leaving behind everything we possibly can.
Getting out is easy, but how you get back in—
say, through a locked window
into a room and a dead love affair
you abandoned the night your future called—
blue moonlight, vinyl floor, lots of mice,
and three creeps in bed—that's different,
so take it easy and forget the lot: Karl Marx,
the parasites and the greedy lovers
and run out into the beautiful life
that awaits you. Goodbye.

12

Love is the most awkward game to play. Love
you, and all the wrappings of repair. Move away.
Hate is something closer to the bone, the crooked shank.
Loving You is what the singers say
crying with a mandolin accompaniment
all the way to the bank. Peace has a symbol
like a dove without a cage, and victim to the hawk.
'The olive branch is easily bent,
and rhyme can very sweetly clothe deceit.'
So he, ingesting a drug late at night
in response to biochemical necessity,
constructed a crossword in the shape of an 'Ode
to Genius', in which the legend of a young Poet
screaming in his trendy garret for an ounce of opium
was finally demolished by the smoke
eating into the paint that held his face together . . .
Love is like a dose of vitamins

13

Maybe you've experienced the feeling of reeling in
a tricky fish? Love is like an angler, or his goals,
obsessively preoccupied with problems of the tide
and plotting out his map against the stars
while fingerlings in countless glittering shoals
play Doctor ('Look at mine!') beneath his keel.
When you're in Love, is that the way you feel?
Love crawls up and knocks you out
and takes you for a ride. While the poet
casts about for the frightful tribes a cold
current is working against him and a vast
tide of frigid water trawls the river bed, stirring up

muddy images and loose packs of themes with needle teeth,
and far across the Pacific, deep in the clouded waters
a movement coloured with despair is working its way
toward the coastal battlements. A sudden squall slathers
ice across his face and in the shrieking wind it seems
that the dead cargoes of all the oceans in the world
swing up groaning from their silty bed and rise
dripping and glistening with phosphorescence
into the unbearable metal blue of 'Night on the Waters'
where the sea's face is glazed with deathly light
and the poem's promise thunders on the broken coast.

14

Nonetheless I am still too young, or
younger than I was, and it's due to a course
of brain-expanding, or younger than that diary
you can see reflected in my dirty window that explains
everything that's gone wrong with civilisation—
it's a forgettable catalogue of folly and pretension,
it's full of gloom and agonised regret and triviality,
it's like a radio play on television, it's like
electric bath-water spilling out of the beach house,
it's more like Mario Lanza than Frankenstein,
though more like Frankenstein than President Kennedy,
and less like President Nixon than a quick fuck.

15

Only ornithologists nowadays write of
blue feathers on a gelid sea
of placid blue, if colours as they theorise
have love of value relatives and ambiguity

and hues are touched with empathy until
they glow with the real uh comparison
of a blue feather on a lake of blue
feathers gelid in the mood of their own unconcern
and 'hating' each other—imagine! hatred tones!—yet
we are stupid because of our binoculars,
our blue spectra and dioptric Ultra Violet
or some other feminine plumage of the 'gelid sea'
so we take a fizzy pill and jump to sleep and
straightaway we become tired in the exhausted
air of our comparisons, and so depart.

16

Perfection of 'the word' whatever
that is, the *oeuvre* of numinous lunch gastronomics
abandoned in mid-choke and throttling on the floor
'like a small and desperate animal'—what can you
make of us, who are so deprived? That we simply guzzle
sound, experience and meaning and are thus disposed
to throw it up? No? That all we mean
is parallels and trizzy metaphysics,
metaphors of loss, we 'quiet ones' who have lost
nothing worse than life assurance premiums?
We who have swallowed 'the best that Western Literature
has to offer', and shat the lot out on the lawn?
Or do you propose to give us holidays
in which we can brush up our commitment?
Plump the flabby pillow of our means? Load one bullet,
spin the chamber, squeak and tickle the trigger and thus
create a new beginning for the literature
of the cultured market gardener and his gleaming wife?

17

Queer, isn't it, how holidays decline
around the rim of a bowl of ratty soup
just so that you and Caroline can make the jump?
And sorry how the idealistic strivings of the young
dribble to a plebbing tack of politics
and tropic mud. But that's the knock, you'll learn to
love it in the end, you and Caroline and Princess
Froth, you and Lady Artemis Gorilla
Sloppy Makeup Throttlegut and all her tribe.
She dives about with copywriters, pokes her tongue,
and giggles in the pool like a randy teacher.
The hi-fi gear is glowing orange with the blues
and Doctor Threat is rolling up your sleeve
for that final pin-prick into yesterday. So choose:
piggy-back the dealer while he teaches you to grease
up that pole, and hope you reach the Muses at the top
and hope you get a good and literary fuck
and if you're nice, a fifty-dollar note. Or get the shits,
hike out through the desert with your awful luck
and take your chances with the butcher's slippery chop.
Look at the snappy camera. Say cheese.

18

Reaching the excuse for verbal intemperance we find
the best argument persuades us to strain out from poverty
to excess, though the profit of this striving
is not in the final chapter but in the zooming
between two worlds of action, neither being of interest
without the gasping towards the other, which is the circus
where we get whatever valuables we come across
and it is not 'reality' nor 'art' that keeps us hot
but the idea of 'hurtling', down the road between

the promise and the thrilling now. This
argument reaches its senility in poetry
for Yeats is said to have composed his most valuable,
fine, and enduring works in flatulent prose
then waited for the scalpel of his intellect and sense
to prong them with the magic clang of verse and wham
bingo they became lasting works of art that students
still can hardly take for granted like a lemonade.
So we end up with a mass of words far more
enduring than a pub bore and twice as sickly,
and our argument smashes through the window
like a trembling ballet dancer scared of rape
but less afraid of broken glass, as we are more nervous
of the poem that might not wriggle into sight
if we declined the challenge of the technique
of cooking 'prose' first and then stamping out
these frilly 'poems' with all their endearing
and 'necessary ornaments of sense'.

19

So there's a dance, and in its alcoholic daze
the Dervish fights his drunkenness;
there is a song whose chords restrict the throat
as music ought. He enters the Gateau d'Ivresse.
It's his Seven-League Boots, this phrase:
'The gangster and his moll'. They meet,
and pass the parcel, and retreat.
'Love? It's just a passing phase.'
Pleasure fits the pockets of his coat.
Slow guitars collect within his gaze.
Dolls, dull stilted birds, a raw
laugh in a jar, the rusty gun.
When the band breaks up his mawkish whore
collects herself. The cheap dance craze is done.

20 (after RD FitzGerald)

These are not restrictions, but equipment
for use in experiment or exploration
such as it is well to have in hand
when leaving main roads for open country, though
often thrown away in side tracks that lead into
dead ends. Moreover tradition is not just an impulse
out of the past; it is a progressive movement
overtaking the present and helping carry it
into the future. To step aside from tradition could be
one way of being left soon in some small corner
which the present has already deserted. But poetry itself
always sorts out the poets it requires
and gives the best of them their orders;
so despite the monotony of much that is formless
the very incoherence and craziness
of what you have to say are not restrictions,
but machinery capable of jacking up the present tense
and marching it along like a heavy sandwich
into the slobbering mouth of the future.
To step aside is one way of avoiding the collision;
to leap into some small corner is another, though here
in the smog of underlying discontent you find
the older Captains shuffling through their orders
as a paraplegic fiddles with his fly,
and this is the activity of mind
out of which poetry and coloured drinks erupt.

21

Undo the past. 'One must be absolutely
modern.' Sure, we can abandon sense
and sensibility, and all the disinterred Romantics
like a wicked boy punching in a stained glass knight,

we can be witty partly because of our vodka slingshots
and that's enough to kick the European jukebox in and
get a laugh. But this 'building' thing, this Bildungs-
roman-à-clef, and forests foaming with the puppy love
of seasons . . . this is architecture, friend, and masterful;
we gape to find the cathedral of words so large
that everyone can find in it the works of his favorite
period, and yet you can always strip that work
of ill-framed accretions and their polyphonic noise
without pulling the whole thing down. Is it plausible
that 'strength' lies in age and British feats of arms?
Are these bits the 'real' cathedral? They might have been,
the whole might have been designed by one man and
finished in the one compelling style, but
'The whole has rather grown than been made.'
Here the jungle is tugged this way and that by armies
of depraved monkeys, for we have reached quandary's end,
surely, as such things have a kind of existence that is
almost midway between the works of art and those of nature.

22

Very moving and persuasive, and too bad the focus
is entirely wrong. To get close enough to grapple
with the problem that lies beneath the problem
that there are no new problems you'll have to crawl
behind the frames in filthy rooms where monsters
fear to think about breakfast in case their hearty
breakfast has eaten itself, and that's nothing
compared to what you'll find behind the scenery,
for surfaces are like chrome in that they rust quickly
and must be scraped away and plugged with fiberglass
thus no mechanic leaves a plane simply polished
but he must have his nightmares confirmed
in flame and crash disaster for lack of digging

into the art of the internal combustion engine, though
we are more like the damaged pilot in his new psychosis
and shall always worry the flight plan to shreds.

23

We could point to the poem and say 'that map',
the heart's geography, and words enact
the muscley parable of exploration: on your right
Maugham's club foot which tromps the clay of life into
a lovely chorus line of English prose; on your left
the dead Romantics, gone into that same earth
that took their tears and all their unforgivable
syntactical mistakes. The land is cruel
with existentialists, though lyric poets
wander through like crippled birds . . . but this map
is false and crazy—here the Doppler shifts
convert to analogue then back to pulse-code modulation
information full of news and noise, so the heart's
continent abandons form and drifts out into the night sky
full of parachutes, and we feel the mind's mountains
bumping against our head like knobs,
for the little 'heart' grows 'dark' at night
and lacking infra-red photometry and radar
we rave down along the flare path looking like
an anxious moth, don't we? In the flight plan?
But there you go again, plotted out of your simple wit
and this is the second-level problem: observers
without the keys to fit their own responses
so that a poem is merely rhyme and meaning, or a gift
of gaudy trash, and nothing else. So we slog on
to navigate the fading resonance of our capacities
and find the luminescent map of armies
burning on the plain.

24

X-ray breakfast waits for the man who rises
quickly: it's 4:27 a.m. and I'm thinking about
time: life is a mouthful of barium and it's 4:28 a.m.
outside the streets shake with snow pneumonia
it's 30 below and I'm thinking that perhaps poetry
used to be the shot that flung the faulted bone
across the lens, huh? or maybe that penumbra
waiting for the Treatment at 4:29 a.m.
and so forth. It's hard to find a purpose
for that grey machine they wheel in in a sheet.
The time runs out, for 'oranges', asking
who needs the teacher? who needs the magazine? now that
we have the movies and can sit drooling . . . cobalt milkshake
waits for the thinker who would think his thoughts
deserve the ink they wish to buy. Go on, go out,
be a good guy and buy some 'oranges', get a 'drink'.
I guess I wait around for the Impossible Profile.
Batman! Batman! (the 'Impossible Profile of Desire!')

25

Yet, as the Legendary Profile conforms to a harmony
then falls away from melody to a broken music
you will find a deep attachment to this taste of absence,
against your will you'll be disturbed by the
persistence of the Profile of Desire as it takes on
an enigmatic pertness you could hardly have guessed at
and it will do you no worship to strive against it
for the Profile is more like the tide in its pacifism
and in its bountiful excess as the paradoxical music
develops a lust for the beauty of the ocean and brings
your reachings into disarray for love of its silhouette,

for the Legendary Profile has haunted generations
and brought cities to ruin by its ideology and though
its glance is thrilling, though it seems to love you deeply
you will find it loves all the cities it has conquered
for a short space of time and showers them
with an air of melancholy that is never dispelled
as its nature is to be more elusive than sympathetic,
and though you may hold it in your hands briefly
it will depart again for its working is mysterious
and has a logic like that of holiness
in its frenzy; thus your deeds will have no peace
and your slumber no tranquillity until the Legendary Profile
is brought by you again into the terrible wasteland
it once inhabited and shall now always inhabit
in your grief, by its absence, by its beauty, by the fact
that its piercing sorrow is forever unattainable
once you have touched its lips and faded off to sleep.

26

Zero is the shape of the volcano's orifice
as seen from above, as it is of the human's as seen
from below, and this witless natural joke is a clue
to the purpose, function and economic value of art.
Something like a nothing is what we find
the final port of call on this cruise when,
stained and weary, we get a flash like a light bulb
blowing up in our face and right there and then
we know everything about life and the creative process.
First there is an accumulated substratum of fact,
and second a kind of thermal pressure built up
over decades of suppressed fantasy. Third,
when the whole thing explodes you have an eruption
and millions of gallons of stuff pour out

into colours of hot orange and vivid green,
material which may be revolting and even deadly
at the time, but which forms a useful ground
for supposition in later ages. And so
while the first burst is primitive and spontaneous
after the style of the Romantic gush of the early
nineteenth century, the later consolidations
take on an air of careful structuring
like a policeman blurting out a list of filthy books
in perfect alphabetical order. And that is all there is—
once the Romantic Emotion has ejaculated we find
a vast bed of cooling lava, bare and empty,
giving meagre nourishment to those who follow,
and baneful and pernicious in its influence. And yet
we are still laughing in the jungle, and this
dream of art is nothing but a loony fantasy.

27

After all, we had left poetry behind before this trip had even begun,
and all the while we have been bereft of its silly promises of beauty,
as the liner leaves the dock and one sees wavelets, sodden stream-
ers in a thousand colours, and some damp flowers drifting down-
ward through the clouded water to that harbour mud; it is as
though the coast of South America were never to see us again,
and as much poetry as we were able to hint at left as a blur on the
horizon as a temporary sign, the more beautiful for being the more
easily erased, and even this has strength as it is inevitable and what
we have been promised and it is one promise that shall come
through: that the slate of verse shall be washed clean, that the
South American rivers will drift always to the sea, that the flowers
in the mud live and breathe for a short time only and then return
us to our dreams.

From *Crying in Early Infancy:*
100 Sonnets 1977

Starlight

Just under the water sheet you can see
dim grass photographs, two prints
coloured to the temperature of glass
that glint from one sky refraction to another.
Between the surfaces a reluctant prediction
for an invisible childhood, damaged by the future.
Under the glass and the broken starlight
the water stained with darkness

soaks into the earth. Somewhere below
a portrait is moved slightly
by a wish or a failure, to form
omens that point into the past
and indicate 'That promise, how
a tiny growth drains all your effort.'

The Bus

My eyes go pale as I grow old, and these
bones, my wrist, are less eloquent than
country radio. I re-live youth asleep
and leave it behind at dawn. In the mirror
there is only me, grey and mumbling.
Who else was in that darkened bus,
driving six hundred miles to a new school?
I should remember those boys, but

those are photographs, and anxious men
inhabit them; nervous wives cry themselves
to sleep in the country nightfall. The moon
shines down on the uninhabited mountains.
The mirror clouds over.
The bus speeds through the forest.

The Chicago Manual of Style

The Chicago *Manual of Style* is really neat
when your composure cracks and ghosts
of silly girls come whispering to bother you—
this happens late at night—just kids
out for a bit of fun with a convertible
and a bottle of vodka like in a movie,
and 'Hell,' you think, 'did I do that? Was I
involved with that mad young bitch

the cops were after down at Sunny Point?
Was that me in Dad's truck with the throttle
stuck open, cracking ninety down the beachfront?
With that . . . brunette . . . uh?' Just about then,
on the edge of love and terror, the Chicago
Manual of Style appears and takes you home.

Art

He was a living legend. He had built
some great structure mainly consisting of art,
though most of those who went through the experience
were knocked around and were inclined to talk about
'a work of skill' and 'admirable diligence',
and thus quite missed the point. Words, paint,
craft, are easily bought, though hard to sell.
Some said he made a million dollars, though

the figure varied, and by the time he got it
he was too far gone to add it up.
Did he really make a work of art?
Did it 'work'? Is it really 'art'?
Is he still alive, or does his 'spirit'
live on in the elegant reviews? Hard to tell.

Artefact

To solve the problem of art and artefact
will you go down to the river
to paint a 'painting'? Will you 'paint'?
Will you paint the girl by the river?
Will you make a painting of the girl?
The light is Grecian, is adequate, et cetera.
He is sitting by the water. No,
he will not paint the girl by the river.

The girl is an artefact, the problem
of the painting is an artefact, is art,
the making of the painting is a problem.
Will you paint a painting of the artefact?
The scenery is well composed, the light
is Greek, is adequate, et cetera.

The Moated Grange

It's bad luck with a coughing baby
and it's just as rough inside the pleasure resort
so don't bother with the Mandrax any more.
You'll get to sleep, and find a business there
that you'll just have to get used to once again.
These palaces you build, or auditoriums,
someone forgot to put the windows in and
all night long you're troubled by a noise outside

so that every day at daybreak you find yourself
asking the keeper 'Was that me? Was that
me and my trouble again?' And he answers variously
according to the weather, 'It was a flock of birds,
sir, of red plumage,' or he guesses 'That, oh,
that was you again, sir, pleading to be let in.'

Ballistics

In a distant field, small animals prepare
for sleep, under the huge rising moon.
For foreign peasants, dusk is none too soon.
The bombers fade into the melting air.
In a far harbour boats make for their mooring,
in another town the citizens are glad
the lights are going out. The morning's bad,
the waiting news is cruel, the job boring.

A painter pours a cheap and bitter drink
and drinks it down. His hand's unsteady;
on the table brush and pen and ink
lie scattered. Half his work's no good,
the rest is sold for rent. He's ready;
the loaded gun discharges as it should.

I Know a Man Who Lives in the Dark

I know a man who lives in the dark.
He writes in black ink on black paper.
Whatever he writes is wonderful.
He thinks about history. At midnight
in the light from an ultra-violet lamp
he begins to write. The book will be read
by schoolchildren, he decides, and politicians,
and he considers the struggling republics

and the joys of a country childhood. He paints
a picture of raw youth forged into a legend,
a terrible landscape informed with a sombre glory;
but the ground is a turmoil of combat whose name
is murder. Musing on the republic's favour
he writes a manual on the implements of death.

The Doll

My daughter's playing with her bloodstained
doll again. And the wireless is breathing unevenly
in Frank Moorhouse's novel, grieving that the old
petrol stations are unattended, that all the decent
Rotarians are missing in action in Korea,
the only war to feature the Sabre,
the modern exemplar of warfare,
and the ruthless MiG. It's goodbye to the glue

that used to hold everything together,
it's goodbye to the trembling Rotarians
and their bereaved children in the light
of stinking kerosene lanterns, it's goodbye
to the countryside of honorable rifles.
Welcome the doll, the terrible doll.

The Spy

The spy bears his bald intent like a manic
rattle through the street. A bitter rain
stains the cobblestones. A clock stops; elsewhere
winter tightens up its creaking grip.
Why does the soldier pace the empty field?
Whose war is this, so grey and easily spent?
Slow cars patrol the autoway, children
stare at you cruelly from behind an iron gate

and a brutish gathering begins, somewhere
on the plains far in the hinterland.
The black clock has been still for a hundred years,
and no peasant bears the luck to win
in this poor lottery. Dull green trucks roll out
and the countryside is well advised to be empty.

Position: Poet

A gift to stir up fevered passions,
in a fit to envision a disastrous future
and to tell it as explicitly as possible,
to see through others as clearly as a mirror
but not to see yourself at all,
this is your basic equipment. As for the rest—
compass, map, a traveller's phrase-book—
use them only if you have need.

You have been provided with a wife and child
and a passport, and a respectable position
with a firm of publishers in the city.
As for the stammering, the occasional
failure of nerve . . . just do the best you can.
Oh—pencil, paper, one-way ticket. Have fun.

The Painting of the Whole Sky

The theme of the magnificent painting
concerns a boy groaning under the weight
of callous governments, and a troop train
moving off to the front. As the train
moves towards the regrettable border the boy
unveils his grief—a whole sky,
storms, and loads of bleeding cloud—
that is his only story, and he cries.

That is to say the train and the wounded
meet like ships in the night. One soldier
loosens a bandage in the wind as the trains
pass in opposite directions. The canvas
flutters, the dried wound freshens, the boys
wave blindly from the painting of the whole sky.

The Blues

I'd like to throw a fit at the
Sydney Opera House and call it Rodent.
That's what separates me from the herd.
The hand forgives the cutting edge
for what the hand guides it to do.
The knife has no pleasure in it.
I'm eating my way through my life—
they said it couldn't be done

but here I am in the Palace of Gastronomes
crazy about the flavour!
Moonlight along the blade of a kitchen knife
belongs to the ritzy forties, it's nostalgic
like playing the comb and one-hundred-dollar bill
and calling it the blues.

1968

As you get purchase the hate vehicle
you take another quick look at your sister
and the whole cataract falls into place
under the idea of economy at sea
along the edges of the truck
your sister is playing around smoking
with a nudist drinking pot just
having a real bad time in Jamaica

you know you'll make naked friends
in the twilight you're not sniffing glue
between the Principle of Uncertainty
and the invention of Germ Warfare
there you will find your dazed sister
purchase motor conformity.

By the Pool

James Michener thinks of writing a guide book
to Bohemian Balmain, Sydney, Australia.
People are sick to death of the South Pacific.
He quickly flies to Balmain and has a look.
There it is, like a movie! Writers, artists!
The harbour, blue as always, the container wharves
just like it says in the novels, and the lesbians . . .
My God, the Lesbians! Bohemia Gone Mad!

This is too much for James, and he flies out.
TOP WRITER JETS OUT OF SYDNEY, AUSTRALIA!
But is that how it really happened? I like to think
of James in the Honolulu Hilton, older and sadder,
nursing a drink by the pool, nursing a broken heart,
dreaming of a pert little lesbian in Balmain.

At the Laundromat

How lucky to live in America, where
supermarkets stock up heavily on writers!
Thinking of the famous poets floating home
to that luxurious and splendid place
inhabited by living legends like an old movie
you blush with a sudden flush of Romanticism
and your false teeth chatter and shake loose!

How it spoils the magic! In America no writers
have false teeth, they are too beautiful!
Imagine meeting Duncan in the laundromat—
in America it happens all the time—you say
Hi, Robert!—and your teeth fall out!
And you can't write a poem about that!

From *Dazed in the Ladies Lounge* 1979

Ode to Col Joye

You open your eyes and realise
it's the morning of a summer's day in Sydney
and it's going to be—not a John Betjeman day,
though you can hear church bells
      faintly across Annandale,
and not a John Forbes day, though
the first thing you notice is your suntan lotion
on the dressing table beside a beach towel
decorated with a crude scene of coconut palms
      and a jet bomber
pencilling a faint vapour trail
      across the Malayan sky
                no,
not one of those days, and you think about
      the exact shape of your headache
and the taste of the first disprin of the day
and you wonder if it will be fine or cloudy
      and then
the hollow yet insistent sound of a Coke can
      rolling along the gutter
fills you in—
          it's a *Ken Bolton* day!
               and,
as if to underline the accuracy of the hesitance
of your mental sketch of an approach
      to the definition of the day itself
a paperboy shouts something like
               New York!
   New York!
   (you're not sure . . . perhaps 'No Work?')
   and when you get up
wearing your shortie pyjamas
      you find a note on the kitchen table
          on a sheet of blue and white paper

to say that Bill and Kerry have gone to the beach,
  and after that
a lunch party at Anna's, hard-edge
  coloured cocktails!
to which *no one* will be invited! you
        gasp
as the water gushes
      cold out of the shower—
it's enough
    to be having a shower
        in the hot
blue summer morning in Sydney, an ambience
that no Melbourne poet will ever appreciate,
  and you almost
blame them for that! but 'blame' is very
  un-Sydney, so you
smile and finish your shower
having adjusted the warmth of the water
  thinking of Bondi Beach
and of the poets you know who will not be
  planning to go to Bondi today, after all,
    they never do, but
at least one of them will be planning to
  write a poem
about not going to Bondi!
      and it's perfect!
as perfect as a milkshake at the Bondi Pavilion
whipped at exactly the right degree of chill
  to get a froth up—a skill
that no Brisbane poet will ever
  comprehend—
    whoops!
      you slip in the shower

but regain your balance, and that too
      is a metaphor!
that no Canberra poet will ever endorse,
                           and
in a leisurely and very Sydney way you write
with a soapy finger on the wall
      of the shower recess
an alternative version of Laurie Duggan's
      'South Coast Haiku'
            a 'North Coast Haiku':

> *The milk can*
> *falls off the back of the truck*
> *crushing the Bonsai Marijuana*

      but you condemn it immediately
for being too
      political
           and the shower does the rest—
                       no,
it's not a Les Murray day, though yesterday
Doug Anthony's name was all over the news-stands
and you found a mysterious copy of *The Land*
on your porch, bleached by sun and rain;
      and it's not a Bob Adamson day,
           though last week a bank robber
ran amok and was shot to death just
five blocks away, under a windy Sydney sky
full of light and utterly lacking in remorse,
      as Melbourne skies are never
           lacking in remorse
and it's not a Poets' Union day, though
last Sunday was full of bickering relatives and
      nothing much got done,

I guess that was a Poets' Union day,
        though it lacked a 'chair'
we have a 'chair' today and I'm
        sitting on it
                it's not
a Sandra Forbes day, though the light is so
pretty as to be truly beautiful in a very 'Sydney'
        and 'cool' manner,
and yesterday I read a poem by Auden ending
        'I love America,
so friendly, and so rich!' and I thought
it must be a John Ashbery day, though 'John'
is hardly 'friendly', though perhaps
                                'rich'
and rather too 'American'
                        it's the kind of day
where I notice that my Renault—
        a beat-up Renault; how
                Sydney, and how French!—
has the name RENAULT on its side in chrome letters—
how metonymic
        that the name of the object is seen as
being part of the object to which it refers
it's a day for writing
        a self-referential line like this
and getting it done in time for a coffee
        and a Chesterfield filter cigarette
and watching the smoke-ring blur
        in front of the window
                like a circular argument
                        about Mannerist art
as confused as the smoke now
        dispersing from the window

revealing a view of—
                    yes, it's *Sydney!* and a
small figure in the lower left-hand corner
crudely sketched with a Faber 4-B pencil
          and labelled KEN BOLTON
is gazing through a window at the viewer—
          yes, *you!*
and from his sternly-thinking head issues a balloon
with the words
               it's a
                    John Tranter day
not like last Monday, for example,
          which was serious and very
                    Alan Gould, or maybe Kevin Hart:
a stranger in the bus said severely
          'I ran into Wilson the other day
               in the Common Room,
and I gave him a piece of my mind!'
(in my pocket there's a postcard from Martin Duwell,
a volcano rising from the sea near Reykjavik) 'I'm
          an Anglican,' the stranger says
and you notice the way the light gleams wetly
          from his glasses
'but I'm not your average gutless (. . .)
          (obscured by traffic noise)
'No!' he says loudly, 'I'm
                    committed!'
and his friend looks at him as though he were mad—
          the Anglican, not the friend, though
he looks a bit funny, too—maybe
          it was really a Don Chipp day after all,
wherein morals, politics and literature
          commingle

like the ingredients of the hard-edge cocktail
that Ken is now drinking with an obviously
        'non-committal air', thinking
'Maybe it's a failed Rodney Hall day,
        that the earnestness of the air
is inadequate to sustain . . . '
                                but it's not,
it's a day for writing something 'fresh'
        for *Surfers Paradise*
and that makes it a Col Joye day; that,
        and the bright air
glistening with poetry and the desire to please.

The Un-American Women

One, they're spooking, two, they're opening letters,
three, there's a body at the bottom of the pool
labelled 'Comrade X', and you've been asked to
speak up truthfully or not at all. It's like Einstein
lolling on the lawn—somebody *gave* him the telescope,
he wouldn't 'buy' one—and our investigator has him
trapped in the viewfinder. Albert! Tell us Everything!
We won't blame you for the Atom Bomb! After all,
you're dead! Four, cancel the code and burn the cipher.
It's no laughing matter when the shit hits the fan—
why are you grinning like that? Are you now
or have you ever been a woman? That's a tricky one,
I know you'd like a stiff rum and coke and ten minutes
alone on the patio to think it over, but
the G-Men in the back room are getting anxious;
the Mickey Finn's invented, the hand that
feeds you's quicker than the eye, and in a wink
the powder's in the drink! Our Leader's dozing
in a tank, and in his memory we labour mightily.
Are you a German Jew? We sympathise; do you?
The Memory Bank is sad tonight, it's asking
for your friends, they have a future there.
Let's share a pentothal and take a ride;
the garden's full of Government Employees
but I'll hold your hand. You make a movie,
I'll write the dialogue: One, we're laughing,
two, we're breaking rules—I'm finished, you're
dead, and as the cipher smoulders on the lawn
a cold glow rises from the bottom of the tank:
our Leader starts to speak, and so will you.

The Revolutionaries

Look in the mirror: everybody's gone,
the black limousine dwindles down the drive
and vanishes, leaving a twinkle in the bushes,
or was that a gun? Do you think we were
invented for a future that failed to happen?
The make-up fits us like a second skin.
Open the tequila, let's drink up and get dizzy!
We've just arrived and unpacked, and you're
smoking reefers, you were always too eager . . .
now you're measuring the drowning pool!
Let's use that ice-pick for a paperweight,
and bring him coffee on a tray . . . a white
stucco wall, cactus, a venetian blind,
a zebra coat of sunlight on the bed, and you
dolled up in orange lipstick and a new print dress!
But why are we here again? And why is the camera
staring at us with malignant eye? The hot lights
go suddenly blind and the blood-stains disappear—
we're back in the 1940s and the surly Mexicans
are crowding at the door, it's all over!
Why am I laughing? I'm watching my obituary
develop, like a stain across an army map—
now they're cheering—somewhere in the crowd
a news photographer loads his magazine—now
they stop, shocked by the gunshot; and then
the numbers flutter from the calendar . . . one last
dip in the pool, darling, and a quick drink—
tonight's the Premiere, and when our future
flickers into life we'll take a deep breath
and walk out into the sunlight, free at last.

Leavis at The London Hotel

You need the money—your way of thinking's
going out of fashion, and you're growing old.
You need the make-up, and you need
the wake-up pills before the bombing run;
the flak is active tonight, you need
a glass of something sparkling and a deep
breath before you're ready for the fray.
On your way to the affair in the back seat
of a taxi you catch a face in the mirror—
bandages and a black eye, is that really
you? It's not Humphrey Bogart—you
should have gone to Acapulco like
mother said, but no, you had to take
the youth cure, then the bandage
loops across the screen spelling out
'Mad Dog', and you guess it's true.
The shark pool looks inviting
when they turn out the lights,
but that's for after breakfast—
breakfast on the terrace with the Krazy Kats,
after the test of strength. Say goodbye
to the Kodachrome mirage and the heavy
petting, from now on your career
shrinks to a point and your many enemies
gather like a gerontology convention and
whisper. After the Monkey Business, after
a famous middle age there's nothing left
but the engines turning over, the crew waiting
in the moonlight—and when you take off
the shadow on the speeding tarmac drops away.

Sartre at Surfers' Paradise

I've been lonely for years, writing in the attic
and I owe myself a treat, so I get anxious—
really anxious—and then collapse—I mean
relax—and *you're there!* No, it's an optical
illusion, I'm cruising for a bruising down the
rue Mort—you don't know me yet, me with my
gift wrapping hiding a heart of gold—*holy
shit!*—there's a beatnik party, it's the
'Speed Readers' rehearsing for their graduation—
look—they're turning into Acid Radicals . . . no,
nobody's reading, and they all look healthy
despite the exceptions and the junkies and
the speech that threatens: we're us, you're
you, singular; it's *that* kind of party, and
I get a hot flush when the cutest kid
on the team screams 'I'm Teacher's Pet!
I'm *Okay!*' and the students argue:
Is Rum & Coca-Cola a new duet,
or a dialectic? or a way of dropping
cheaply through the floor of the visible world?
They sing: 'I wrote a letter/ to my friend/ and
on the way I dropped it . . . who/ picked me/ up?'
Not the strobe, not the psychotherapist, not
the existentialists cuddling in a corner,
not the girls flashing like a double negative
that argues till the group takes off . . . it's
'Karl Marx and the Moonies' and I'm anxious—
you're not there among the optical illusions
and the female impersonators—anxious
but happy, dancing in the dark.

Foucault at The Forest Lodge Hotel

Your good taste is so packed with reading
you can hear a coin drop at fifty paces, but
is that how infatuation heats up to the pitch
of lust? With a trick flame and a gas tank?
General Paresis and a pack of cronies
are practising the Blitzkrieg Variation—
'A frontal attack on the Lotus Eaters
and you're home and hosed.' Our guide
to the good life is a drunken junkie, half
girl, half executioner, breathing gas, who
fucks like a disco wizard and exemplifies
sheer speed as a final virtue, eating out
with a rush: that's how tonight develops
into a drug catalogue blazing in the
waiting room where I get a crush on
Suzanne Pleshette and in that flash
rise like a broken bottle into the light.
The mob of men, dazed in the Ladies Lounge,
inhale a bright idea: *We're* not slack, we're
paralytic! For twenty cents and a wet kiss
you can take a gun and kill an alien invader,
for a dollar you can overhear a fat man
mortified, but this is only the rehearsal: by
midnight the loonies have arrived, hand in hand,
it's the real thing raving with a purple head
and a bossy affection for noise. The jukebox
plays 'My Foolish Heart' over and over, then
breaks, and I get emotional again—we're
smoking in the hotel carnage while our future,
thinking deeply, waits for the music to begin.

Enzensberger at 'Exiles' Bookshop

At the back of the bookshop a karate expert
keeps a pot of coffee brewing, in the window
a man exhibits his bandages and the lights
flash red, amber, blue; all night long
the sex magazine quiz gets filled in.
What am I doing here? That cloud layer
threatens nothing, and speaks casually
of a distant beach; everybody's laughing—
they trained beautiful men and women
to meet me at the airport, they
follow me around and buy me lunch,
they point out the misfits and the deviants
and keep me amused at parties where young men
fight and make up like emotional Brownshirts.
In Martin's Bar the topless waitresses
are all sober, their perfectly matched tits
jump at the drunks while upstairs
a poet listens to the race results,
next door at The Balkan a cloud of burnt fat
gushes up the ventilator; these
are the good times, Australian style,
this has become a new vernacular
and waits for my typewriter to turn it into German.
Europe is a ruined Paradise buried under
books; here, nothing important was promised.
I'm drinking coffee and writing
in English on a piece of crumpled paper;
soon I'll learn the native dialect and ask
Where are the ovens? Is it true that you never
learned to kill each other? Are you happy?

The Wind

'Due to the shortcomings of indexation
all new equipment with technology changes
will be black banned.' CMX Videotape
Editing NECAM Audio Mixdown wind rushing
up the empty stairwell no one home
Telemation Character Generators Optro-Desk
Digipatch Lighting Systems the telephones
ringing in deserted offices no one at work,
hangover holiday—'E.N.G. was introduced . . . without
any prior notification' the traffic buffeted
Digital Delay Slave Units fluorescent lights
fluttering off, floor by floor, 'The best editors
of my generation have resigned for spurious
and often politically-motivated reasons'
in Studio Control the lights are out, only
the glow of the meters and the red, green
and amber push-on push-off buttons on the desk
reflected in the dark glass wall the actors
wandering home through the windy alleys
at the back of William Street 'You have returned
at an inopportune time to an organisation
bereft of any semblance of morale . . . ' the light
shudders continuously in the Listening Room
Check Meter Ballistics and Azimuth Malfunction
a Turbo Porsche throttles up the street
knocking down a kid, television floats belly up
a balloon of bad dreams, the editors have gone
to bed with other people's angry wives
under the scattering wind I look for fragments
of a better life

The Germ

'There's a huge germ behind the glass—
break it, and a terrible plague
will decimate the galaxy!' As he spoke
the Commander grunted agreement. 'You mean
one in ten of us . . . will live?'
'No, die,' came the answer. 'Okay, take a break!'
The director curls up in a corner
and dozes off. He forgot his tablets, and dreams
again about the huge germ eating all his money.
The script girl goes out under the cold stars
for a coffee and a good cry. The glass wall
of the Control Room looks like a mirror,
to the film crew, under the lights; or
history, thinks the sleepy director, the history
we want but never get. 'You making enough money?'
'Sure, sure.' The lights go up, *clack clack
clack.* 'You mean you're in *love* with him?
With *that* bastard?' The script girl's crying again
and the shooting has to stop. These tiny emotions rise
and fall, and many things are changed forever.
'Jim! I can't do it! The Voltage Gate . . . *aargh!*'
'Listen! You're an alien, aren't you? Well, *try!*'
And yet the history mirror presses against them, and
struggle as they may, the germ is inevitable.
'Nice take, guys! Wrap it up!' They pack up the gear.
'Goodnight!'
                    'Goodnight!'
                                    And far into deep space
in a drifting starship, the aliens turn off the video.
'Some movie, huh?' The crew break out a bottle
but the Commander goes to bed. He has the nightmare
again, about a germ, and a decimated galaxy.

The Great Artist Reconsiders the Homeric Simile

He looks back over the last metaphor
and his eyes shift their focus, his gaze weakly
taking in the litter on the desk and then
the blurred garden, its order and composition:
bare trees, a path strewn with leaves,
a distant figure dawdling at the gate—
light dazzles the window-pane with brilliant
diamonds of dew—he sighs, and drops his pen.
As when a detective in the spring has found
a junk-struck hippy crouching in her pad
at the dead end of Desolation Alley, and
has faked the evidence and booked her, soon
her man returning giftless from his rounds
sees the flat empty and his girlfriend gone;
at that he freaks out, and checks his stride
and with short uneasy steps circles the block,
with smothered groans repeating her name; but she
lies on the cell floor, overdosed,
a heap of bright rags—never again
will those disco mirrors catch her image
floating by, nor the bathroom echo her
withdrawal screams—as that poor addict
hides in horror till the heat cools off,
nor knows his loss, so Matthew Arnold brooded
on his failing similes. His cup of tea
grew cold as he stared out at the autumn
leaves; a change of air was what he needed,
a holiday at Dover, or Torquay . . .
and as he mused, the lounger at the gate—
the Future—turned his back, and walked away.

From *Selected Poems* 1982

A Jackeroo in Kensington

With a fistful of dollars in a knapsack
and a brutal turn of phrase, colonials
are crashing the party. *Cette parade sauvage—*
on the skyline you can see Rupert Murdoch
crawling over Fleet Street, a pygmy King Kong—
did they shrug off an empire for this?
Too right, boss, that's what I want to hear,
the glib, slangy lingo of the tango dancers
steaming into Sydney Harbour in a sepia haze—
it's the bottom of the world,
say the blond sophisticates. Hang on;
wasn't 'King Kong' invented in America?
The eyes that look into Australia
are European eyes, Peter Porter said, but
my friends' kids holidayed in Hollywood,
and live in San Francisco. I'm
middle-aged, and England made me, cobber,
reading Maugham in the shower recess—though
what about Malraux? and Lao Tzu?
I'm going to be a Chinaman
next time around, speaking perfect English—
or Creole—who can choose between
the torrid charms of the one and the
cool, pragmatic bite of the other?
Can you say *You fuckwit!* in Italian?
No way, but if you play Wagner
loud enough you'll get rich quick—rich
in the Bloomsbury sense of the word—
a humus of culture, a knack for sleeping in,
these things adorn you like a froth
and the National Gallery opens its doors
for you, and you alone, at last.

From *Under Berlin* 1988

Backyard

The God of Smoke listens idly in the heat
    to the barbecue sausages
speaking the language of rain deceitfully
    as their fat dances.

Azure, hazed, the huge drifting sky shelters
    its threatening weather.
A screen door slams, and the kids come tumbling
    out of their arguments,

and the barrage of shouting begins, concerning
    young Sandra and Scott
and the broken badminton racquet and net
    and the burning meat.

Is that a fifties home movie, or the real
    thing? Heavens, how
a child and a beach ball in natural colour
    can break your heart.

And the brown dog worries the khaki grass
    to stop it from growing
in place of his worship, the burying bone.
    The bone that stinks.

Turn now to the God of this tattered arena
    watching over the rites of passage—
marriage, separation; adolescence
    and troubled maturity:

having served under that bright sky you may look up
    but don't ask too much:
some cold beer, a few old friends in the afternoon,
    a Southerly Buster at dusk.

Country Veranda

(Dry Weather)

This country veranda's a box for storing the sky—
    slopes, acres of air
    bleached and adrift there.

From outside, a shade-filled stage, from inside
    a quiet cinema, empty
    but for the rustling view

where a parrot scribbles a crooked scrawl of crayon
    and off-stage a crow
    laments his loneliness

and six neat magpies, relaxed but quite soon
    off to a General Meeting
    stroll, chortle and yarn.

When the summer sun cracks the thermometer, laze
    there in a deck chair,
    shake out the paper

and relax with the local news: who won the cake
    in the Ambulance raffle;
    what the Council did

about the gravel concession down at the creek, who
    suffered a nasty fall
    but should be well in a week.

(Rain)

From that open room where sheets hang out to dry—
    cool, wet pages
    whose verses evaporate—

you stare out at the trees semaphoring their sophistry:
    their tangled, pointless plots
    and obsessive paraphernalia,

drenched among the spacious palaces of vertical rain
    where no phone rings
    and neighbours are distant.

Behind that ridge of mist and blowing eucalypt tops
    the world waited once:
    exotic, inexhaustible.

You've been there now, and found that it's not much fun.
    On the veranda, silence
    fills the long afternoon.

North Light

He looks around his son's room: the bed
unmade, the globe of the world with an
imaginary voyage plotted in blue ink,
the clutter of books and plastic toys,
a life gathering its tackle together and
pushing forward. He stares at the backyard
and the thick bushes growing upwards.
The only movement is the glitter of leaves,
and the washing his wife hung out,
before she went to work, flapping
in its circus. Something you can't see
holds it all together. What is it? Last
spring they painted the house: amateurs,
but doing the job as best they could, then
they laid bricks in a pattern in the yard—
what is it, that makes the pattern hold?
That party where they squabbled, the dinner
where old friends got drunk and happy . . .

He sits at the kitchen table, half dressed,
drinking a glass of orange juice,
and wonders about the delicate adhesive
that holds it all together. Once, long ago,
he'd been divorced: a sad, frightened drunk
living in a rented room.
                            When the washing's dry
he'll gather it up, in armfuls, and bring it in.
He turns on some music. The house has a
northerly aspect; it is full of light.

Widower

Moving among the dull red glow, which
stands for the darkness behind the eyelids,
he drifts like a sleeper, deftly making dreams
manifest. A brief beam of ghost-blue,

then the developer, rippling. This alchemy
to which his once magnificently complicated
life has shrunk, has filled his daylight hours
with its chromed gadgets and protocols.

In the evening, in the secret room scented
with expensive chemicals, he conjures up his
darlings again: a girl with hair the colour
of the tassel on the corn-cob she's holding;

and his wife—so young, in her fifties frock—
waving from an old red sportster that somehow
looks brand new. He stares and
stares, his face swollen with longing.

In the rest of the house one or two lights
have been left on, as though a family
were sitting up late, talking, or perhaps
listening to the radio, together.

Debbie & Co.

The Council pool's chockablock
with Greek kids shouting in Italian.
Isn't it Sunday afternoon?
Half the school's there, screaming,
skylarking, and bombing the deep end.
Nicky picks up her Nikon
and takes it all in, the racket
and the glare. Debbie strikes a pose.

In a patch of shade a grubby brat
dabbles ice-cream into the cement.
Tracey and Chris are missing,
mucking about behind the dressing sheds,
Nicky guesses. Who cares?
Debbie takes a dive. Emerging like a
porpoise at the edge of the pool
she finds a ledge, a covered gutter,
awash with bubbles and chlorine's
chemical gossip. Debbie yells there,
and the rude words echo.
The piss-tinted water slaps the tiles.

Debbie dries off, lights a smoke,
and gazes at her friends fading out
around the corner of a dull relationship
and disappearing.
                  Under the democratic sun
her future drifts in and out of focus—
Tracey, Nicky, Chris, the whole arena
sinking into silence. Yet this is almost
Paradise: the Coke, the takeaway pizza,
a packet of Camels, Nicky's dark glasses
reflecting the way the light glitters on
anything wet. Debbie's tan needs

touching up. She lies back and dozes
on a terry-towelling print of Donald Duck.
She remembers how Brett was such a
dreamboat, until he turned into
somebody's boring husband. Tracey
reappears, looking radiant. Nicky
browses through an Adult Magazine.
Debbie goes to sleep.

Voodoo

From his rushing-away, from his
ever-receding throne, under a rainy
canopy of trees and scraps of cloud
that topple back, shrink and disappear,
embalmed behind his rear window in a nest of
crushed velvet plush, the flash wog's nodding dog
blinks out his witless approval to the vehicles
that shadow him forever.

His twin the dipping bird sips and sips,
tilts back, cools off, dries out,
dries out utterly, totters weakly
on the lip of philosophy
then dips again.

These two critics teach us how to live,
rehearsing the gap between the no-no
and the drink-again. Their motto? Every day
I will get better at embroidering the lingo
of the tongue-tied doctors of letters; every night,
in the lack of light, I will get better
and better at the negative virtues, telling
girls to piss off, who needs them,
swimming off the edge of the rock
ledge into the plunging broth of deeper waters,
soaring up to the stratosphere, bothering the angels
and yarning with God. My left hand writes it,
my right hand tells me that it's right.

In the pre-dawn rack and bash of winter peak hour
traffic on the Sydney Harbour Bridge you notice them
hefted up over the city like ju-ju dolls
in the trance of a terrible gift. You note
the man with gauntlets and the goggled girl
on motorbikes, the nurses' giggles
in the fogged-up Mini Moke, an ambulance weaving
and howling in the rear-view mirror, the tablets
rattling in the Emergency Bucket, the icy rain
furious and seething on the road, and Noddy
and his loopy brother brooding on it all
for our sake, so that we can see it whole.

Fine Arts

Beyond their exhausting vanity and their hatreds
the Old Masters agreed in the small hours:
a work of art, they said, collectively,
        lies in a kind of mud:

gossip, bad faith, someone else's
wife, phone bills, a little happiness. And so we
go on, they said, doing what we can; while
across a horizon full of exasperating detail
        a headache piles up.

And yet the swimming pools are full of children
laughing in that deafening sun, and the barbecue
gets assembled. In the long afternoon one marries,
        one plans a divorce.

Are the Old Men right to maunder, taking young love
as a sketch for heaven on earth? The hot spring
fevers burn away the bossy mannerisms, bringing
complex couplings: some in beds, some on the telephone,
but mostly delirious: is this possible?
        Is that right?

An emotion as perfect as a painting hangs over Sydney.
In the shadowy cave an apprentice, humming
quietly, colours in a background of traffic
while the Master stares through the bright doorway
        lost in the visible world.

The Creature from the Black Lagoon

Sunbathing on deck's the done thing,
but it makes the Brylcreem run
and stain the collar of your poplin
beach shirt. Palm trees drift by
as though your sins had turned vegetable
and semaphore. Sins of the laboratory, I mean,
not the confessional . . . yes, the engine room
looks suitable, and through the porthole
a wise old man waiting patiently
in the wavering water—that's no priest!
Captain! But the Captain's a gutless
foreigner, drinks gin, and never shaves.
You pity the girl in the bathing suit—
she may be a palæontologist, but
sure as eggs she's going to get
a terrible fright. And the ethnic extras,
they have to die on our journey
towards the knowledge that shimmers behind
the South American façade.
                                        The priest
turns his scaly back: that creature,
rising like a new disease from the gene pool,
why should we pity him? Deracinated,
maybe, but what a guy! No, it's wrong—
don't kiss him! I can feel it,
soaking through the blood-brain barrier . . .
he's never known the touch of a woman's . . . whoops!
Here's the nut with the speargun on a hunting
spree—Duck, Tabby! Duck and cover! Here comes
the bolt from the blue, to shut up sorrow,
to stop up the barrel of fun like a dead
king.
            And what colour's the blood, Doctor? Red?
Can you explain that? And what of the offspring?

High School Confidential

1

Remember blotting paper? The Year of the Pen?
Pen, I mean, not roller-ball. Come on, gang—
you guys—applied to girls—those teenagers,
they seem to have disappeared, behind
a fit of the giggles, or a hot flush.
One minute they're practising the drawback,
confusing innocence with ignorance, then
you look into the glass and they're all gone.
Did they just fade out, bathed in the glow
from a fifties movie? Did the girls all wear
plaid? And ponytails? Hey Butch,
let's have a pillow fight . . . outside,
a snowfall blankets the small town.
The crew-cuts, the red and green
chequered shirts adorn Dad's jalopy
bumping away from the zone of focus
like insignia stencilling a boundary
around their tribe and epoch.

2

TV holds some fascinating specimens, sure thing,
an endless museum that seems stranger and less
human the more we gaze at it through the faint
reflection, glazed on the screen,
that reminds us of someone important,
though it seems to play possum: one face
layered on the other, related somehow,
across a mysterious dimension that never moves
yet through which all things move
towards a common grave.

Stratocruiser

This is a dream I had each night in Korea,
where I was very busy killing in a plane:
I boarded an ocean liner as my destiny
ordered, and sailed away. The sun came up
over the scented tropics, day after day.
Then the underbelly of Europe appeared:
its black ice, its suffocating manners.

And then I was nodding off in the bar
downstairs in the Stratocruiser—
endless thunder over the Sea of Japan,
droning home through a mile-high wall of rain—
you wake up just as you think 'touchdown',
and the fat tyres kiss the wet tarmac, bump,
shriek, and touch again.
                              The flak jacket
waiting to be invented, your shabby suit
hanging at the cleaners with another name
carefully printed on the tag—your roles
were there all along, shifting slightly
in the shadows of a doorway somewhere in
South-east Asia, but still yours, and you
slip back into the last half of the century,
unannounced, unmarked, without a second look.

Laminex

Staring through the steam that clouds the window
of Abdul's Pizza Bar on King Street, you reconstruct
Newtown—the Newtown of the rag trade avant-garde—
as the heat ripples rebuild the traffic.
The teenage dreamers cruising their torpor
for a cheap hit mean less and less as
each one scores at Serafim's Ephedrine Heaven and
drops off the planet, another click on God's
calculator—if only you could give it back
to the street, the way the street deals it out—
and then, with hardly a flicker, you're aboard
the Lavender Bay Ferry glimpsing Paradise,
1963: the Beatles rehearsing 'Twist & Shout',
a Luna Park sunset in faded Ektachrome
unspooling on a screen at the back of your mind,
the moving finger spelling out a lucky
number, the suburbs as close as a giant
face against yours, breathing, while utterly
elsewhere she's waiting in the Persian Room
tapping her nails on the laminex. Once
you were growing up through sunburns
summer by summer, in those leafy backstreets
full of parked cars. Then—it happened invisibly—
you were loafing on the dusty edge of Australia
or soaking in a tub, becoming fashionable
reluctantly, like the cigarette papers Dad used
that now endorse a more nitric habit.
The steam fogs the glass, and Abdul wipes it
with a cloth that's filthy, but it clears the view:
she's there, frowning, as the magazines taught her,
against a background of drifting pedestrians.

Lufthansa

Flying up a valley in the Alps where the rock
rushes past like a broken diorama
I'm struck by an acute feeling of precision—
the way the wing-tips flex, just a little
as the German crew adjust the tilt of the sky and
bank us all into a minor course correction
while the turbo-props gulp at the mist
with their old-fashioned thirsty thunder—or
you notice how the hostess, perfecting a smile
as she offers you a dozen drinks, enacts what is
almost a craft: Technical Drawing, for example,
a subject where desire and function, in the hands
of a Dürer, can force a thousand fine ink lines
to bite into the doubts of an epoch, spelling
Humanism. Those ice reefs repeat the motto
whispered by the snow-drifts on the north side
of the woods and model villages: the sun
has a favorite leaning, and the Nordic gloom
is a glow alcohol can fan into a flame.
And what is this truth that holds the grey
shaking metal whole while we believe in it?
The radar keeps its sweeping intermittent promises
speaking metaphysics on the phosphor screen;
our faith is sad and practical, and leads back
to our bodies, to the smile behind the drink
trolley and her white knuckles as the plane drops
a hundred feet. The sun slanting through a porthole
blitzes the ice-blocks in my glass of lemonade
and splinters light across the cabin ceiling.
No, two drinks—one for me, one for Katharina
sleeping somewhere—suddenly the Captain
lifts us up and over the final wall
explaining roads, a town, a distant lake
as a dictionary of shelter—sleeping
elsewhere, under a night sky growing bright with stars.

On Looking into the American Anthology

1

In California a young man is stuffing a briefcase—
first a jug of light, the words 'water'
and 'stone', a blurred image of a guy in a pickup
    truck with a gun

staring through the hush-squeak, hush-squeak
of the wipers, a frail woman, crying. A leaf, a sob,
a clod of mud. There! His class awaits the real,
    the Deep and Meaningful.

Driving downtown he sees a pair of jugglers
inch up the face of a glass cathedral full of
marriages, mirrored in the noon glare, one on top,
    and then his double.

The neon signs in the suburbs full of graves say
'Giants Drank and Died Here'. Autos, rusting trucks,
police helicopters roam restlessly, their motto: Do it
    First, and do it Fast.

2

Down here in New Zealand, jet-lagged in transit
at the bottom of the planet, a clutch of
Flight Attendants giggle in a corner: one gay,
        the others married.

The sun that has looked down on Hollywood,
on lust, Las Vegas and the will to power,
rises, *rhododactylos*, on Auckland Airport:
        through the tinted glass

a perfect field of fodder, five sheep,
a tractor nosing at the sedge, the shrill
cacophony of jets rehearsing like a madman
        staring at a vase.

Nothing the amusing natives do here matters
in the Capital. The giant engines lift us
through the sky. The next stop—Australia—
        is the end of the line.

Shadow Detail

You press the bakelite button, and wait,
and wait. Presently the lift rattles
down to the ground floor, and the attendant
passes you something through the brass grille.

The chlorine sifts down through the water,
turning pastel blue. That woman floating
fifteen feet above the floor of the pool—
she's taking medication for weight loss,
a cheapskate pharmaceutical that stretches
and compresses the day until it disappears
into the hot white dot in the centre
of the screen. The thin man in the
viewfinder acts like an instructor—
'This is the patented exposure guide;
snap it open and look at the sunlight.'
Overhead a bumpy plane—a two-tablet bomber,
the man calls it, shading his eyes from the late
afternoon glare—laboriously scrawls a message
on the haze that tints the sky pink.

At last it's evening, and a chill breeze touches
the lawn. Now they're all staring at something
resting on the bottom of the pool. At least,
that's the way you read this photograph.
The shadow detail builds up, telling us
about their hair, the boy's dark tweed jacket,
pointing out details, the texture in the
broad masses. And the ancient lift creaks up
to its cage at the top of the building,
a cage the wind visits and teases.

Parallel Lines

1

parallel lines
autonomy, then breakfast

as if the coastal light were perfect
perfect in its tonal range and balance

let's have a slide show (Kodachrome)
and impress the (American) neighbours

meet Kathy, burst into tears,
a list of things to see and do

things I hope will make me happy
happy, not miserable

post blotto triste old chap
all animals are perfect

2

intersecting lines
astrology, then breakfast

the weather's just right for the
multi-coloured debris of bodies

imperfect notes, the Latin scribble
bottled deities

I trust them to make me powerful
at least, less anguished

3

we meet at last, old friend
I think you're enlightened:

the world climate has arranged itself,
do you realise that?

its power is really its needs, not
unconscious needs, but not conscious, either

good at night, bad in the morning
I wish to live to a great age

4

I think you're stoned again
or is that true love?

my need, my lack, is powerful
a malignant spirit, bad adaptation

but subtle and wonderful drugs . . .
Bayer, Merrell, Roche, et cetera

I'm grateful for those children, but
why do they get lost and angry?

dig deep and be generous
for your own sake, said the book

5

that horror's maladaptive
'suffering demeans'—Somerset Maugham

failure of light at the end of the day
racing to finish the artwork

as the sedative descends
onto the vast delicately-coloured beach

live by the water, the fellow said
it's nice to be smart, but not enough

this pretty hologram you won't need
at the end of the road.

Having Completed My Fortieth Year

Although art is, in the end, anonymous,
turning into history once it's left the body,
surely some gadget in the poet's head
    forces us to suffer

as we stumble through the psychology of it:
the accent betraying a class conflict
seen upside-down through a prism, the bad luck
    to be born in a lucky country—

yet in the end it is our fault, i.e. my fault
not to be born Frank O'Hara and cursing
a whole culture for it—it's no excuse
    not to be run over at thirty,

to live on, turning out couplets
with the fecundity of a sausage machine
but without the cachet of the Imperial drawl,
    not even a cute lisp;

above all to miss out on drugs and Sodom
in the mindless mid-afternoon heat among
the nylon swimsuits and the beery surfers,
    a trial, not a vacation—

the girl around the corner gagging on whisky
in the schoolyard after dark, the boss
clocking off and weaving out the back door:
    'I'll be at the pub . . . '

well, at forty, the pieces lie about
waiting to be picked up and puzzled over
and fitted into a pattern, after a fashion,
    one I'm not fond of—

there are two sorts of people: those who say
with an owlish look 'There are two sorts of people',
and those who don't; then there are the writers
    who live on another planet,

their droppings bronzed like babies' booties
and we're glad to see things so transmogrified
though we suspect that life's not always rhymed
    quite as neatly as that,

and then there are those for whom every voyage
is an opportunity to lash the rowers,
the sun rising over something absolutely
    dreadful every day:

a people totally given to the cannibal virtues,
a set of laws designed to confuse and punish,
an art that shrinks experience into a box then
    hermetically seals the lid;

but squabbling over Modernism won't help,
England needs liberating but not by me,
she has concocted her own medications after all
    for marsh fever and the sinks,

so I'm stocking the fridge with Sydney Bitter,
checking the phone numbers of a few close friends
while the conservatives see to it that I conserve
    my sad and pallid art

and I'm hoping that the disk drive holds out
at least till the fag-end of the party
so my drunken guests may go on bopping till they
    drop into their mottoes

as I did some twenty years ago,
embarking on this yacht, this drudger's barge,
being 'absolutely modern' as my mentor taught
    from the embers of his youth,

and hardly guessing then what would turn up:
these postcard views from a twinkling and distant
colony, of the twin cities: dying heart of Empire,
    sunset on the Empire State.

Boarding School

Bright gods, trust me to play
the game properly. Meeting you
suddenly, I think you're tops;
I'm absolutely riddled by lust

at least I think it's lust.
In the morning the room is cold.
I mutter under the silver rose, alone,
gaping at the disappearing universe.

Breakfast matters: you're there.
Is it love? Look out, bossy-boots,
some among us have been thus bedevilled.
Bothered thus, I natter, happily.

At the coming-around of the clockwork
and the gathering-in of the rosters
the chatterers remember everything;
the whole dining room is lucid.

The daylight passes in a daze of weather.
We're imperfect, but that's perfect.
In the dark we'll be truly happy,
as animals are, my precious.

I'm tall and clever, but is that
enough? I'm only an amateur, and
I don't want the pillow talk.
Turn on the darkness. Impress me.

Papyrus

Look at Egypt, sunning itself. We
took the camera; now sit on the stool.
The pistol is full of blanks.
Don't speak French, whatever you do!

Rome, O Painted Whore, you are a sight
for sore eyes, or for our attempts
at abstract art, the billy on the boil,
prison gas leaking outside

the walls. Is it rat poison? I'm
wearing red silk for my passions,
the priest said. It cultivates them.
Kids kiss innocently, like cocoa butter.

I'm spelling dirty words out
for the girls. It's easy. Like
he was tossed on the wave
passion drowned him under.

I am restless for your
. . . skin burning . . .
touch!' A grass fire
and . . . fever . . .

[married women] . . . *hetaerae*,
their kisses
and . . . [cried out] . . .
were . . . [broken] . . .

After the Dance

Someone has raked the driveway smooth,
someone has turned the porch lamp on, how
thoughtful. Small town nightfall: young folk
gather for the old-time dance, the ligatures,
     the bonding rituals.

Comb your hair, sweetheart, your Prince
has come. On the gravelled river-bed
weeds are plaited together the way
we are entangled, pussy-foot, in a
     dance of destiny.

The picture of a wheel spinning makes you dizzy
as the frame emotions skid out of sight. She
thinks she's making me happy, ha, have a drink.
Where they flash the two-coloured dog
     the speeding stylus writes.

I see the Roman pens moving in the gloom,
they flex, they make me powerful, malign
stars glitter and rain down, they won't stop
The storm . . . learning . . . bodies, tangled
     . . . struggle for love

curtains lazy close beach flood
broken bridge at the end of the track. I watch
. . . river swollen . . . can't help what this
Towards the future this pretty . . . marriage
     small town . . . catastrophe . . .

Haberdashery

Hey, you there with the scented lipstick,
take me to the bosses and their club,
if they exist, these functionaries. I love to
flirt with money, and the idea of large money
writhing in a bundle under the weight of politics.
Cleverly spoken, Debbie, you're a top girl—
are you on the loose? Hmmm, looks good. But . . .
catching you, I'm catching someone else's germs.

Our hostess and accumulator of lies,
presiding at the barbecue, her looks astray,
catches two wives in a warm embrace,
how can they help it, their husbands utterly
rattled in the face of their girlish needs,
they're so bright and I'm retreating into headache.
I'm all knocked up, this moody weather. Shame,
mechanical in its operation, a real shame.

From each emotion manager, wrote
one of the husbands in a last attempt,
frowning and clutching his head, *to each
worker in the factories of passion* . . .
but the salesman of love had lost his touch,
and in the foaming pool each foray discovered
another girl wearing a blank look of bliss.

The hostess watches me. Am I her only male?
Snappy dresser! while others to a feast depart
hence from regiments of the unhappy
while the busy host was getting drunk.
Then he and the girl tried on the same size
dresses and the chatter dispersed, two or more
of the shop assistants crazy about her.

Poolside

The host climbs out, soaked and spitting oaths,
and a teenage girl leaves the barbecue.
Two of those drinks your wife mixed,
bright pink and cheerful, and I'm
seeing double: breasts, twin headaches
exactly the same size await me
frowning from each temple, and a diptych
concusses the chatter: a car salesman
hitting his better half. A pygmy politics emerges
wherever two or more of you are gathered,
shopping together. All right, stop biting,
I'd much rather sleep with you than with
that other poltergeist. You're greedy,
aren't you? O Painted Laugh, why is your
belly convulsing? Can 'a man' become a sign
for 'a muscular spasm'? Horoscope,
betray yourself, take me back to a feast,
if this is a feast, these glib flirtations,
the whole gang badly knocked out
by the mundane speech the flame attempts,
each sleep a cancelled cheque, as I
watch myself thinking of you, deracinated
Sweetheart, boarding a Greyhound.

At The Newcastle Hotel

The last sunlight filters into the bar
      through the bottle glass:
a green drink in a green shade . . . that's
how the country's run. Great Calculator,
      lighten this burden.

My little number, bless her soul, she's
      safe at home in the suburbs.
Unravelling her cares, the pink rinse
Den Mother ravishes the Armchair Bolshevik,
      and the spent executive.

Your spouse, Smiler, was in here a while ago,
      looking pretty crook,
her nerves shot to pieces, reminiscing: a young
girl, old times, rock on the idiot box
      making your nerves jump.

Well, they were the days, of course.
      Time flies, old son.
Another one for you, Kevin? Well . . .
One more gin and tonic for the lady.
      Time, gentlemen, please.

Affairs of the Heart

Affairs of the heart, they say.
Fortunate, those who can care.
Print the body count, the harm alarms.
A spare personality begins to spin

out of control. Their bodies, then their minds
aspire to more before darkness, can
damage more domestic love than all
animal hatred may. This doesn't happen.

Is this madness what it's about? This
slipping, breakage, she hopes repair can't
be long away. Kissing brings ease.
Beware, they dream, the thirst of lips.

Spin faster, delirious stars.
Pining won't help, so let's begin
snooping about, caring a little, loving
again, all those ridiculous things.

Lullaby

I'm not jealous of your pet executives—
their coma therapy, their new guitars.
The latest boyfriend's hardly seventeen,
isn't that what the tabloids say?
In the cheap hotel, the heaps of magazines—
You Can't Go Back to Woop Woop, sobs
the big print. And the speed jerking
up the spinal column to its spasm above.

Now the sea heaps itself on the pillow
with its wacky promises, and you're floating
through the ceiling again. Tell sex to go
back to the playpen where it came from. Your
future's waiting: suburbia loud with radios,
telling you to wake up now, and do the shopping!

Dirty Weekend

My husband doesn't know and wouldn't care
how smart you are, pretty boy. How did you adapt
your fuck-truck style of driving to a foreign car?
The way you dress, the deep looks, how painful.
A paint job, murmurs the sea, skin deep;
mid-life crisis, says the fashion magazine.
Is that shack a motel? Really? And
the local champagne, so ethnic . . . see how
the small town dies in the dead of winter.
They are embalmed, the grey, the soon-to-rise:
a shopping spree waits behind a wall of money
for its casualties, and you, blond sparkler,
with your sunlamp tan and sleight of hand
are a token passed between women. A breeze
speaking of summer, tinted Serepax Pink,
blows in through the screen door
and a naked couple rise groaning
out of their sweat—they're animal
dreams, in the mirror, aren't they?
floating into my holidays. Yes,
I'd like to be indelible, a perfect bruise.
Down here at the bottom of a whisky glass
you're staring at the bill, waiting
for your jackpot to fall out of my mouth;
you should know better, cheap trick, but then
you're new to the game, aren't you?
Here, clothe your idiot wishes in a
fifty-dollar kiss and let me sleep that
dreamless sleep that's more a kind of grieving,
then watch me haunt your future, blurred,
half erased, like a red tattoo.

La Pulqueria

The dance floor is the threshing floor. The next day
she gets up at dawn and carries a string bag
along the arroyo, looking for the spangled motto
that will win her father the holiday prize. Then
flame bursts from the shower instead of water.

He opens the safe—under the sacks of cash
are glass phials filled with pale blue tears;
evidence that the garbled speech of the poor
is rich with hidden meaning that only their priests
have the key to, and they're keeping mum.

The lovely widow is sweeping the courtyard;
an agile young man drenches her with promises
from the lime tree, then from the balcony.
He grins as she drinks the *pulque,*
and it spills over her blouse. She stumbles!—

She's skinned her tits, ape-face! Knockout
drops . . . the thick green glass tumbler
bounces across the linoleum when I faint and drop
everything. Now she wants to go rowing
on the lake, the water sprinkled with stars.

Thus God teaches us a necessary astronomy,
recharging our batteries for the dance.
When I kiss you, the lovely young woman says,
*the planets rotate like a tractor threshing
attachment—now will you marry me?*

From *The Floor of Heaven* 1992

Breathless

It was an autumn evening, after a meeting
at Masterson's; four of them stood on the steps.
'I could do with a meal,' Hunter said;
he really wanted to talk more with Sandra.
'Florenzini's is the only place in Sydney,'
proclaimed Lovelock, a young painter
with thick red hair. 'What do you think?'
Sandra—thirties, clever, a pretty blonde,
wearing a plaid skirt and sky-blue top—
agreed enthusiastically: 'It's just the place.'
So they set off down the darkening street,
with Sandra and the painter striding ahead
and Hunter and Mr Tennyson Lee following.

If you'd told Hunter he'd spend that night
in the arms of a self-confessed murderer,
drinking gin and listening to Billie Holiday
singing the blues, he wouldn't have believed you;
but as it happened, that's where he ended up.

Around them the Australian economy staggered
under the assault of various foreign banks,
and crowds of workers lately turned into their
doppelgängers shopped angrily, consuming
what they produced in a different incarnation.
It seemed that the contradictions engendered
by the anomalous lifestyle of the urban worker
were producing a kind of psychic acid,
and it rained around them in a thin mist.
'What do you think of this dago dive,
Florenzini's?' Lee asked Hunter,
as he kicked aside a small terrier
tugging on a tartan lead. Its owner shrieked
and shook a fist, but was soon left behind

in the tumult of confused but purposeful shoppers.
'Are you fond of the Italians, Mr Hunter?'
'I hardly know the place,' Hunter yelled
over the thunder of a passing truck.
'I haven't seen much of Sydney since—
oh, ages ago. I'm a bit out of touch.'

Crossing against the traffic, Sandra stumbled
in her high heels, and a motorbike
almost knocked her down. She shouted
at the rider's disappearing back—the noise
of the revving engine made it hard to hear
exactly what she'd said, but for a moment
Hunter thought she'd shouted an obscenity.

At Florenzini's they huddled into a booth
near the front, where they could look out
through the misted glass at the pedestrians
struggling in loose herds through the rain.
The restaurant was old and dimly lit,
the walls covered entirely with paintings—
all badly executed, Hunter thought,
student work, apparently, from years ago—
and the crockery was chipped and motley:
'Newcastle Hotel,' said a dinner plate,
and a cup and saucer claimed the parentage
of the Victorian Government Railways.
They ordered bowls of the thick spaghetti
the place was known for, and a bottle
of the appropriate cheap red, then,
when that was gone, a bottle or two more.

  'I think Masterson's a bully,' Lovelock
muttered eventually, wiping the sauce

from his beard. 'Did you notice the way
he hammered Flack, and poor old Sturgeon?'
Lee pounced. 'Rubbish! You speak, my friend,
the product of the bull. Masterson?
A bully? Cruel? Quite the opposite.
He succeeds like a lawyer, by pleading.'

'You've both got him wrong,' Sandra put in,
stripping off her powder-blue cardigan.
'God, it's humid.' She shook her blonde hair
loose. She'd hitchhiked around the world—
Greece, Afghanistan, South-east Asia—
and at thirty she'd gone back to study
something vaguely masculine at night,
Hunter remembered—building, town planning—
and though her voice had a breathy edge
she spoke confidently. 'No, Masterson
is a leader, but his strength is hypnotic.
He hasn't turned his magnetism on you yet.
He can see you're not ready to receive
his insights. Like the wise rhinoceros
in the fable, who refused to be hurried,
he's biding his time. When that time comes
he'll turn the power of his gaze on you,
and you'll wilt.' She laughed suddenly.
She was making fun of them, Hunter felt,
though he couldn't quite see the point.

Lovelock fiddled with his meagre moustache.
'Rhinoceros horn,' he said, 'now there's
a kick. There's a drug to stir your blood,
and turn your superego to a heap of jelly!'
'So you've tried the famous rhino horn,
my friend,' said Lee. 'Was that during your

East African sojourn, the elephant safari
you spoke of so eloquently today?'
'Rhino horn? Is that like cocaine?'
asked Sandra, in what Hunter realised
was a faint American accent. Why hadn't he
noticed it before? 'I'd love to try some.
Do you sniff it? How is it prepared?'
She seemed to be leading Lovelock on.
'Powdered rhino horn,' intoned Lovelock,
'like a certain gland of the marmoset
and a poisonous secretion of the Indonesian
Coral Whelk, is an aphrodisiac, Sandra.
I'm not quite sure that your background
has prepared you properly for its effects.'
There was something pompous about his manner.
Hunter noticed Sandra's mouth tighten.
'What would you know about my background?'
she whispered angrily. Lovelock went on:
'I believe in undergoing all experiences,
so of course I've dabbled with rhino horn.
Once, on the Gold Coast of Africa—'

'Your philosophy cannot be so
immature,' interrupted Lee.
'Undergoing all experiences, indeed!
What of the experience of ingesting
wet cement, pray tell? What of leprosy?
And any fool knows that rhino horn
is not an aphrodisiac. But enough of this.
Sandra,' he said. 'You've hardly eaten.
May I order you a second course?
There's an old saying, that a man—or
a woman, I presume—should eat like a king
in the morning, like a prince at midday, and

like a beggar at night. And look around you—
the women eating like goldfish at all times,
and the men like a pack of wolves. I'd be charmed,
my dear Sandra, if you'd try some
Drunken Beef with me. It would do your blood
a power of good.' Sandra blinked.
                                        'Some what?
What did you say? Did he say "Rump Beef"?'
Lee laughed politely, and touched her arm.
'No, my good lady, I said "Drunken Beef",
a specially of Su Shih's Chinese Restaurant,
whither I propose to take you. This
Italianate monstrosity is overpowering,
it is too much for a tender soul like mine.'
They looked around them. Florenzini's was
hot, smoky and full of shouting customers.
Hunter felt that he was getting drunk.

'I don't know about this Chinese restaurant
of yours,' Lovelock said, 'but "Drunken Beef"
is in fact a Japanese dish. De Quincey
got it wrong, too, but he had the excuse
of being stoned on opium. He claimed
he saw it in a vision—a boiling vat of
buffalo and beer, attended by Malays.
In fact it's a regional speciality of Kobe,
on the Southern Island of Japan.'

'As usual,' Lee said, 'through your arrogance,
you have misunderstood. We have a saying:
"Those who speak cannot listen, those who
listen do not speak." So listen, please.
Yes! I have been to Honshu in Japan where
the famous Drunken Beef originated, and there

watched the unfortunate animals fed, and later
eaten of their flesh. They are nailed firmly
by the hooves to a floor of oak planks,'
embroidered Lee—Sandra went pale—
'and force-fed a blend of corn meal,
Irish stout, and the finest Calvados,
the famous apple brandy of Normandy.
When the wretched animal is plump enough,
it is slaughtered by a Shinto priest,
the meat is hung for the ritual period,
a lunar month, and embalmed in rice vinegar.
It is seared lightly, and devoured as warm
as the Apostle Luke's faith, as it were.'

'By the hooves!' exclaimed Sandra. 'By the
hooves! Oh, those Orientals are so cruel—'
Realising her blunder she went red,
an attractive flush spreading quickly
up from her neck, which was ornamented
with a string of peach-tinted pearls.
'Oh, fuck—I didn't mean . . . that is,
the Chinese, they're not the same at all . . .'
'As you infer,' said Lee quickly, 'the Japanese
are different from the older Asiatic races.
The Chinese, among whom I number
some of my ancestors, are a subtler
and less warlike people. In the East
the Japanese are noted for the cruelty
of their women—a canard, I might add.
There's a folk tale I heard once
in a bar in a jazz club in Shanghai,
involving the faithless wife of a Japanese
rice merchant. This female oaf, one night
during a terrible storm, took into her house

a half-drowned sailor. Her husband was away
in the capital dealing in rice, tired
and footsore—' He broke off here, remembering
the thrust of Sandra's original complaint.
'But you mustn't labour under the delusion,
my distressed and slightly inebriated lady,
that it matters a whit to the hapless beasts
to have their feet fastened to the floor.
Hooves are—how shall I say—integumental,
like the toenail. Done with care—or,
in the case of the Japanese ranchers,
if we can call them that, with skill,
the neighbour of care—performed with a modicum
of skill, it causes the beast no pain at all.'

'You're full of bull,' said Lovelock angrily.
'I don't believe a bloody word you say.
Show me this restaurant.' They both stood,
Lovelock knocking over his empty glass.
'Follow me,' Lee said, and in a moment
they had gone in a swirl of coats and scarves.

Hunter reflected sadly on the bill.
'Let's finish that bottle,' he said.
'I doubt they'll be back. If they do find
Su Shih's they'll try the Drunken Beef,
and if they don't they'll either quarrel further,
or find a bar and try to patch it up.'
Sandra nodded, and he noticed she was upset.
'What's the matter?' he asked.
                                    'Oh, nothing,'
she said, blowing her nose. 'I've been taking
various things to fix a sinus headache,
and they always make me feel a little flaky.

All I wanted was a bit of fun,
a glass of wine, a story, conversation,
something to remind me that I'm human.
And now, a fight, a quarrel, and it's over.
I thought I'd left all that behind.
But you never can, isn't that right?
You've been around, I can tell.
Oh, the things a person can survive, it's
extraordinary, the papers wouldn't believe it.'

She rummaged in her bag and found a bottle,
and spilled a heap of pills onto the table.
They were brightly-coloured, like beads—
red and yellow ones, pale blue and black,
clear capsules filled with rainbow crystals,
a scattering of apricot tablets.
'Eenie, meenie, miney, mo,' she said,
and swallowed one, washing it down
with half a glass of wine. 'You see, when Derek—
Mr Lovelock—talked about his brother
being killed by an elephant in Africa—
that's what threw me, I guess, because
I had a brother, and he died too—
and it was my fault, because of a pizza!'
She swept the scattered capsules into her bag
and snapped it shut. Hunter was intrigued.
'I thought you said you were an only child,
he said, 'earlier this evening—'
                                    'Yes,
that's true, but I also had a brother.
But not any more. I've lost—I've lost—'
She faltered, stopped, and started again.
'Sometimes I think I'm another person,
so much of my life has disappeared.

We were living in the States then,
my dad took us there in the early sixties,
he worked for an oil company, in Canada,
then in Southern California.
I would have been . . . oh, twelve, I guess. Tony—
that was my brother—what a lovely guy—
Mom and Dad were out, and I asked Tony
to get us a pizza from the takeaway place
just down the street. He took the bike,
he had this big Harley-Davidson, God
what a noise it made, he used to
tune the engine in the yard and just sit
and listen to the sound, as though the bike
were saying something he could understand.'
She addressed her handkerchief, and went on.

'Just past the corner near the Dolphin Pool,
half-way home, a Thunderbird hit him, some
rich kid whacked out on speed doing
ninety-five, the cops said, minimum, and
no lights. Poor Tony wasn't speeding,
just getting a pizza for his kid sister.'

'I'm awfully sorry,' Hunter said.
'Things are hard to take, at that age.'
He didn't want to change the conversation,
so he stopped there, and waited quietly.
He had a feeling there was more to Sandra
than she let you see at first—a strength,
a complexity of character, though each new
layer seemed to contradict the last.

'Mom and Dad never got over it. They broke up
two years later. Dad took to drink, I guess.

Mom took to men. And they weren't my parents,
not my real ones. That came out.
When Tony died, they told me. And later,
back in Sydney, I searched through the papers,
and sure enough, there was the story.
I was famous at the age of one.
Tot Survives Bizarre Tragedy, that's
what the papers said. And worse things.
My real parents were religious—
my father was a lay preacher with
the Plymouth Brethren—fundamentalists—
in a bush town miles from anywhere.
I guess we each have to find a faith
to fit our needs, like those molecules
that lock together in a certain way,
but what needs are satisfied by that
loony, punitive rigmarole?
I found out later that he thought
the baby—me—I wasn't his—
my mother had a lover, he believed.
Who knows? What does it matter now?
They were driving fast along a bush track
at dusk, going to some gathering,
the car full of bibles, the papers said.
And—I imagine this—arguing, fighting.
Around a bend, some timber-cutters
were jinking a large tree out of a gully,
and for a few minutes the steel rope
stretched out tight across the road.
Why wasn't there a look-out? Perhaps
there was, and they drove right through,
shouting, quarrelling. God knows.
The cable cut straight through the car,
decapitating both of them. I was

asleep at the time, apparently, in a basket
on the back seat. One of the papers—
I looked it up—said 'Father's Head
in Baby's Basket.' Can you believe that?
Isn't that sick? Who would write
a thing like that?

                'So I was an orphan,
and my other parents chose me—chose me,
I wasn't just forced on them like now,
with adopted babies, incognito—chose me
from the orphans' home when I was one.
Like choosing a puppy, from the dog pound,
to save it from the needle. So, travel,
and America. And Tony's death.
He was an orphan too; his parents
had been killed in New Guinea, in the war.

'I hated America at first, when Tony died,
for what had happened. But I got used to it.
I found a sweetheart, a school romance.
We were too young, I know that now,
my parents tried to talk me out of it, but
how can you talk to a teenage kid? He was
weak, I can see that now, but back then
all I could see was his brown eyes, just like
my brother's, and his kindness. We were happy,
for a while. We got caught up in that
hippie thing; smoked a lot of dope.
We both wanted a baby, but it seemed . . .
I couldn't have one, for some reason.

'Terry—that was my husband's name—he
got into bikes more and more, it was
a thing the Valley kids were doing then.

He'd dropped out of a couple of jobs—
computer programming, office work, then
working in a lumber yard, but he just
couldn't hack it, the routine, he said.
He joined a gang, the Wreckers; I had to
go along with it, I had nothing else,
did I? I had to follow where he went,
or I'd have lost him. Well, I lost him
in the end, anyhow.
                        'The gang leader
was a guy called Big Bob, a pilot,
someone said, in Korea, but he'd
dropped out, like the rest of us.
He had a silver medal that he wore
sewn onto his jacket, upside-down,
that he called his "dead-men money".
He'd been voted leader of the pack,
but you could tell he didn't want the job,
he liked to be alone. He had this hut
where he went fishing in the spring, and
lay about and read philosophy, he said,
but all I saw was fishing magazines.

'A year or so went by—you know, with bikers,
they say they're bad and violent, yet
all I can remember is the peaceful times,
talking, drinking beer, washing up,
like a summer camp, or a family
on a holiday that never ended.
And then Bob had this . . . accident.'
Sandra swirled her wine, and stared into it
like someone who looks into a crystal ball
and sees something awful taking shape.

'We took our bikes out, six of us,
four bikes, for a picnic in the country,
and on the way home, in a valley
in the foothills of the Sierra Nevadas
we came across a flat stretch of road—
the lights of a homestead or two, no traffic,
and the highway like a strip of ribbon.
It was just on twilight, and Big Bob
stopped and looked back the way we'd come.
It was perfect for a game of chicken,
"Blue Angels", they called it—this
aerobatic trick they'd seen on television.
Two bikes would ride off a while,
a mile or so, while the others waited,
then they'd turn back, and both pairs
of bikes would race at each other like—'
she interlaced her fingers— 'like so,
passing one between the other pair,
at ninety or a hundred miles an hour,
it takes a split second, and one mistake,
the slightest wobble—well, you can imagine.

'The darkness seemed to come on quickly—
it was cold, this was in the Fall—
so we switched the lights on—"Go, Drake!"
says Bob, and the other bikes took off,
Drake on one, then Hogan and Maybelle,
and that hammering sound the motors make
faded away down the stretch of blacktop—
it grew quiet and peaceful, just our engines
turning over softly, and I heard a bird
whistling and chirping in the grass
at the side of the road. Terry and me
on one bike, Bob on the other, waiting,

the sunset like a big purple blanket,
the whole world fading into darkness.
You could see the stars coming out,
one by one, like lamps being lit.
The air was so clear, and it was so
lonely there, like the floor of heaven.

'"There they are!" said Bob, and revved up
and was gone in a scattering of gravel.
It took us five hundred yards to catch him.
"I'll take the centre," he yelled, "you
take the wing!" and he tilted the bike
to steer right between the pair of lights—
my God, the noise, a rolling thunder—
except—the headlights, it was a truck
loaded up with logs from Oregon
hurrying to get home to Oakland—
we heard the horn just before he hit,
that sound, like an animal in hell,
howling.'
        There were tears in her eyes,
just visible, but she blinked a few times
and they were gone. Hunter started to speak
then hesitated. What could he possibly say?

Sandra sniffed, then took out a compact
and looked at herself and pursed her lips.
'Worse things happen,' she said cryptically,
and snapped the compact shut.
                'Anyhow,
the second-in-command took over.
Drake, his name was, he was with us
the night Big Bob was killed. He was a
strange guy. Like Charlie Manson,

but not so sick or twisted, or as vicious.
Drake had a strange power over
men or women—anyone, it didn't matter.
Charisma, they call it. Even animals,
he could tame a doberman, just by
talking to it, real quiet, I saw him
do it, to a guard dog in a timber yard.

'Well, most of the gang were just
out for a good time—parties, drinking.
Drake was different, he had a purpose:
sex, drugs, Nazi insignia,
like a religion, only upside-down,
and he kept bullying and pushing.
He soon twisted the gang around.
Some left, the others who stayed,
lost people like Terry and me,
sadists like Hogan, and silly Maybelle—
we were a crew of losers—ragged, dirty,
our minds all slightly wrong.
I think it was the drugs that did it,
that sent us off the planet into space.
I know I'm a strong person, underneath,
but in those days I was out to lunch.
Maybelle disappeared for a week, one time
out in the desert, and came back crazy.
She'd picked up a rich old man,
some insurance executive from New Haven
who was holidaying for a while in Reno,
so she was staying at The Gambler's Rest,
a classy motel way out of town—she said
she was half-drunk and half-asleep
when a purple flash lit up the room,
flooding in through the windows, and

when she went to look, it was a spaceship,
and they took her aboard, and she passed out—
they wanted to breed with Earth people, these
things with large pale heads—so they
put Maybelle into a tank of fluid,
and wired her up, and took out her memories,
then put them back, with a new personality.
They carried out sexual experiments
while she was hypnotised, she said,
and taught her the language that they used
and the history of their planet, blah blah,
then sent her back to wait, among
the people of Earth. Imagine, a biker's moll,
chosen to be an alien John the Baptist,
to make straight the way, in California!
Oh, the things you believe! And Maybelle,
two or three times a day you'd catch her
with her head tilted on one side, like a bird,
listening—"How are things, Maybelle?"
I said once, and she answered: "I'm listening
to the voices in the radio, they're speaking
to me, not to you, so get lost!"
One time from the washing machine,
she heard them, one time in her jaw,
she cried out and said "My teeth are buzzing!
Stop it!" and it was Them again,
talking from a filling in her tooth,
babbling and chattering through the static
with baleful messages, and weird instructions.
Like one time they told her
to cut off her hair, and she did; another time
to fetch thirty pounds of chicken livers
from some bird ranch in Oregon—
God, the smell!—crazy errands like that.

When we laughed at the things she had to do—
biting all the dogs she saw, one day,
washing her hands twenty times, another—
she just shrugged and said: "They're testing me."
We believed it, or we went along,
what's the difference? We were stoned
most of the time, and aimless, or rather
running in a circle after Drake,
doing what he said—there was a lot of
nasty sex—well, I don't want to
talk about that—and a killing once,
at least Hogan boasted he and Drake
killed a member of a rival gang,
but they lied about so many things,
who knew the truth? Our personalities
had been . . . knocked a little out of whack.
I wouldn't say brainwashed, exactly,
but it was close, and we all felt the same—
breathless, waiting for something to happen
that would lift us right up into the air.

'Then the Trek. That's what he called it.'

Just then a waitress came up—'Excuse me sir,'
she said to Hunter, 'but we're closing up.'
Indeed, Florenzini's was nearly empty,
the last few customers gathering their coats.
Hunter paid the bill, and they left—
'There's a place down near the water, let's
get a coffee,' Sandra said—so they wandered
downhill though the rain-wet streets.

Two hundred years ago a creek bed
would have led them to the bay; now

tram tracks and cobbles buried under asphalt
led them under half-lit tower blocks
past locked trucks, cafés shutting up,
pawn shops and fire insurance offices
to the oily waters of the Harbour.

The crowds had thinned out, the streets were dark,
but they found a coffee shop still open
and took a small booth near the front.
They could see the Quay through the glass,
and the last ferries nosing in to dock
and rest on the black, rocking water.
The waiter, in a strange insistent voice,
asked if they wanted a coffee, or—
he spoke lower—or a 'Special Coffee'.
'Oh, the Special,' Sandra said brightly,
and he brought them something in a cup,
a drink that wasn't coffee, but a kind of liquor—
'Vermouth,' Sandra whispered, though it wasn't
any vermouth Hunter recognised—pungent,
dark, and sugary, like a mug of port.

'The Trek,' Hunter nudged. 'You were saying?'
'The Trek was Drake's idea,' she said.
'He called it his Life's Work, he spoke of it
in biblical terms, but when you looked at it,
we were just a pack of bikers on a run.
It wound across the States like a rattlesnake:
Las Vegas, Amarillo, Albuquerque,
Route Sixty-six in the sun
to Oklahoma City, then Memphis—
you could say it was a flight into Egypt—
so we ended up in Alabama.
Drake had spent his childhood there, an orphan,

in this big old house that used to be
a mansion, before the Civil War.'
Here Hunter went to say something,
but thought better of it.
                              'Alabama,
but the backblocks,' Sandra continued.
'Dirt roads, rusting automobiles,
weeds thrusting up through everything,
scrawny chickens running through the grass—
so we ended up one evening
in the ruined garden of the place
where Drake had grown up. As a boy,
he told us, he'd found a tunnel
that led under the main house down
a hundred feet into a limestone cave,
and in a heap of rubbish and broken wood
he'd found an old diary, and a pistol,
and in the diary was a message, he said,
that seemed to indicate that a treasure—
money stolen from the Southern armies,
at the end of the Civil War—was deeper down,
behind a dynamited rock-fall.

'There were only three of us by then—
half the gang had got into a fight
in Memphis, and ended up in jail,
including Terry—well, by that time
Terry and I had broken up, Christ,
life was a mess—where was I?—
and Hogan had smashed a leg passing
too close to a circus truck in Texas.
So Maybelle and I were sitting there
in the dark, holding a flashlight,
an old sack full of detonators,

whiskey, and a plunger dangling a wire
that threaded down into the labyrinth
where Drake was placing his explosives
to blow away the rock—forty-seven
sticks of gelignite—he was bright, Drake,
but twisted, and he had this obsession
about prime numbers—so, exactly
forty-seven sticks, no more or less.

'It was gloomy in there under the moss
and the shadow of the trees; I was brooding,
listening to the crickets and praying
we wouldn't be discovered by the cops
when Maybelle tilted up her head
and said out loud: "Yes, Master!"
Well, I freaked out—"What the fuck
is going on?" I whispered, and she
stared at me with a crazy smile—
her eyes seemed to light up in the dark,
and I believed, then, about the aliens—
"Sandra," she said, "the waiting is over!
Now I know what to do! The plunger,
you have to push the blasting plunger
when They give me the signal. Drake,
They know him as the Enemy of Light,
he let Bob die that night,
we were with Drake when the truck went by,
we saw him guess—the dark, the headlights—
but he made us wait, hypnotised—
his number's Forty-Seven, of years
on the planet Earth, and Forty-Seven
murders among men, his life
has ravelled out its thread, and he shall die.
Wait!"—she tilted her head the other way,

and seemed to listen to the Harley-Davidson
parked beside her in the leaves, the metal
ticking as the engine cooled—and
in the bizarre fright of that moment
I knew Maybelle was right. She said
"Now!" and time disappeared, like a piece
clipped from a ribbon, between the Now!
and the plunger there was no time,
no moment of decision, nothing! Just
the handle going down, and a thump
from far off, deep under the ground.'

There was a long silence. Hunter heard
a fog-horn far out on the water,
and the swish of passing tyres on the road.
It had been raining; liquid pools of colour
cycled through green, amber, red, as
the traffic stopped and started at the corner.
The waiter brought another 'Special Coffee'
without being asked. The stuffy air
was full of smoke; Hunter's heart was pounding
and he felt out of breath.
                              Just as Sandra
started to speak again, the door banged open.

It was Mister Lee and Lovelock, arm in arm,
carrying a bottle each, and laughing.
Hunter noticed that Lee had a bandage
wrapped around his right ear, and Lovelock
looked rather bruised about the face.
'Su Shih is the name, the nom-de-plume,'
said Mister Lee, 'of a friend of mine,
a master cook'—Here Lovelock interrupted—
'Not of Drunken Beef!'—and Lee went on—

'Master cook, a poet, and a diplomat.'
They sat down, squeezing into the space
so that Sandra was pressed against Hunter.
She looked into his eyes. 'Hi,' she said.

A jukebox that Hunter hadn't noticed,
in a corner at the back, began a quiet
jazz trio piece. He felt strangely happy.
'When Su Shih's not cooking, he's
drinking,' said Lee, 'and all the while
composing poems. Here's a lovely one—
please excuse my feeble translation:

> The Harbour flows always to the East.
> Its waters have drowned many lives,
> Many sailors, poets, and gentlemen.
> However sad, the waves keep flowing.
>
> Perhaps these sentiments are silly,
> And I am foolish, with my grey hair.
> Life passes like a dream. So I drink
> To the Harbour, and the Moon, this wine!'

Sandra laughed, her face to the light,
a full clear laugh that gave Hunter
a catch in his throat. Lee opened the bottle
and poured their glasses full. 'To good cooks,'
Lee said, and they drank. Hunter
put his arm around Sandra's shoulder.
The brandy had a sweetness, and a bite,
and a faint sparkle on the tongue.

Sandra raised her glass. 'Here's to
the sailors, the poets, and the gentlemen,'

she said. They drank again. The music
seemed to slacken its tempo, the drums
pulling the bass back, and then the bass
slowing, lifting the piano's embroidery

the way a wave might raise a line of bubbles
into a brief rippling crest of foam—
so thought Hunter, tasting his drink—
out across the cold moonlit waters
of the Harbour, where the last ferry,
its motors turning slowly, made for home.

From *At The Florida* 1993

Journey

The door slides shut with a hiss and it seems we're moving out
    falteringly at first, the brick
    flats tilting then
    reluctantly shifting
aside. We're starting a long journey with half the plot,

some of the story, nothing to worry about and hardly a clue.
    Now a canal's rotating slowly,
    now a sodden paddock, starring
    a wrestling girl and boy.
All gone; we've had quite enough and we're shooting through.

It's hooroo to the broken mirrors and the scraps of sky
    glaring from the wet turf,
    the torn panties,
    grass stains; turn
your back and be rid of the lot of it, say goodbye.

Somewhere long ago you hunted among the chatter
    clutching a damp hand,
    frightened of appetites,
    bold, shaking, wondering
why she wanted you so much, and what was the matter.

And now she's disappeared, or what's worse, turned into just
    another bothered mum. Back
    there in the twilight
    then, she was a pink
breathless angel, all clumsy enthusiasm and lust.

They hope for more, they all want something mysterious,
    the heartbreak girls, the
    lost lads, it's no
    thanks to the bread of life
but give them a piece of cake and they go delirious,

wanting the sun to dazzle and stand still forever,
  youth to ripen, passion
  to flicker and flash,
  every cheating
kiss a puzzle, true love a paradox and a fever.

And what are you doing here? Do you deserve it?
  Dodging the blades, weaving
  between the wheels and not
  getting the chop?
You're hardly the handsome dandy after all, more the nervous

middle-aged college visitor bewildered at tea,
  ashamed of his tie:
  the wrong badge,
  prickly hedge, life
a locked book and an idiot rampant in a tree

wondering what the fuss was about at the front of the hall:
  the shriek, the slap,
  the shattered glass, the
  burst of clapping,
the stock market crash and the shock declaration of war.

And we seem to be rattling out of control along the track
  that clatters into the
  country, turns a bend,
  and vanishes into
the forest, into the waiting shadows, into the dark.

At The Florida

I loved the city like a gift
in the mingled devotions of traffic;
every day I received my own taboo, that
    tactless advice column,
      and a thick mist
covered the carnage, a curtain for innocence.

I'll fidget something up later—yes,
I should escape experience, and do it soon,
but with this brain, this frail
figment fond of light shocks, I guess
I'll stay at The Florida and condone it all.
I can tell you this is the ruin of a way of life.
Basking here I can escape the assembled lessons—

Who was that?—slipping her anklet on,
disappearing by means of a spell and a drink.

My addiction to eucalyptus—the blue haze
    that intoxicates. Here
history folds up once its proper hour passes
and the room is silent, a double berth
you share with your better self.
On the screen the pieces of radar Greek sleep,
and on the walls two mirrors who insist
the heavenly twin was photographed twice.

I guess I'm unlucky, I slipped on the edge of the pool
and saw how venom is blended with pallid talent,
conflict seen inverted all the way down
to the horizon at the bottom where
lights, extravagant chemicals, parties all through
the ever-receding evening blend and gallop,
the new music baking it all in the Arab tongue.

She stands out of my memories of that night
lit by a blue flash, cursing in that
      deviant lingo of hers
the ranks of fun troops,
      the trashy pranks,
someone who wavered in my gaze among
streamers, drinks and black light sparkles,
      fireball aliens nodding off—
we were underwater in a wobbly room,
treating ourselves with a special
emotion developer chilled with ice.

Now the lagoon excursions fill the papers,
and not a week without a new crew from Hartford
or somewhere elegant, each sedan
with a collapsible roof tinted pastel,
with white sidewall wheels and bright spokes.

You mature, or so you think; you become your notes
on epigrams—young love, pale fever flattery—
how it messes up the index—don't suffer
behind the glass, teach for a week,
learn canteen humility, rehearse your chatter.

One day, bright and early,
coffee, a few close friends, she
among them: a kiss, a promise.

God on a Bicycle

for John Forbes

A handful of snow turns into a cloud
shaped like a camel, then a weasel, and briefly
troubles Carlton's sidewalk restaurateurs
before cruising on to Port Phillip Bay
to ruin things for the weekend sailors—
     or is all this just a wish
projected from the forehead of the cyclist weaving
through the traffic outside Readings bookshop?

Soon, he says, he'll return to his true vocation:
icing complex jeremiads on a wedding cake
so the young couple on top of the confectionery
get a bit of a fright before the gin and tonics.

               Right now he's
bouncing off a silver Volvo as it makes the turn
into the driveway of Gino's Gents Apparel—
first you hear the thump, then the car tyres
crunching to a stop on the gravel made up of
countless chips of genuine Carrara marble.

Dark Harvest

Thunder unrolling over the vulnerable city,
purple and ink-blue, above the huddle of workers
scrambling to commute, some to a bar where
    neon and darkness

conspire to enfold them, the avenues alive with shoppers.
And rustling in the wind high above the age of doubt,
their transparent psyches rain-wet, rent by lightning,
    spirits and angels

adrift in the jet-stream know that we have to die,
each of us heavy with hope but a faint shadow trails
between what we need and what's accessible, at noon
    rest and distraction,

nightmares at midnight. For that teacher
boys were everything, once, holding their breath
and proving their passion from a few paces away.
    They can be cocksure,

skin all aglitter, for whom the avenue of blooms
shall never spell 'love'. The drinkers murmur their
ancestors' games, getting it right without
    knowing the meaning,

where to grow through these enigmas means
foreign fucks, sad furious travel, this dilemma:
mud and air, part of the human breath it demands.
    Listen to those guys

rattle and blather, he said, and you didn't remember
that melancholy, the twilight autumn air, then
the rumpled nameless force pushing us out
    towards the horizon?

Garrulous history tells us that greed and ambition
stir the struggle to make great art, but then
the riders gallop up with their strange truth,
    troublesome, painful.

Secretive rumours, but we spoke outline English,
nothing solid, our filthy lies melting into the air.
Buy a memory or two at the pool, who cares if it's
    a little dishonest?

Too bad you only smile to rake back a smile
to crush a truth, or in an instant forgive,
each time shadows falling across the yard, we
    kiss and a heartache

ruins our childhood. Yet—no, though
their cruel trade troubles us, the hot boys
grow, grunt and turn in that awful flux,
    girls become women,

summers diminish, the snapshots fade,
and I remember the neon glow on her lipstick—
these fragments constrain memory into grief,
    baffled and restless,

breezes at sunset bring us groans and whispers;
now the tide is full that will carry us off,
afloat on that glassy flood, the sky stooping to
    touch us with incense.

This is a painting, of a catastrophe cranked up to
the higher range: look at it, sweetheart, you dazzle,
I'm holding you lightly in a dance embrace, watched by
    celestial tourists

drifting above our foreigner-inflected summer.
And our doting neighbours give us what you see,
unwelcome presents, and it's not even an occasion.
        Endless revision,

clearing the discord: there they are, portrayed naked:
two lovers aware of the hourglass–figured space
between us–and the futures they build there,
        reading a novel

one to the other, pulse to pulse signalling
sex, fear and betrayal, culture rearranged
and magically loosened and tightened again,
        deep disappointment,

appalling encounters, garlands strewn far inland,
haystacks aflame in brilliant streaks in the valleys,
and on that sombre green beside the pond
        spirits descending,

calmly alighting in the gloom under the trees.
Here the painter has depicted the world's end, two
plausible powers, the red and the black, demons and
        hard-hearted men sunk

deep in their silent employment, is it for you? And
for you this dismal project, this politics? And yet
the boys still dive and plunge among the foam,
        talking with kisses.

Rising to meet us, the ebony hand of night.
Here, a blur of moonlight. There, rippling noises,
love swept gasping through it. Disguises,
        painting on linen,

it's a delusion and a false fabric, a sweet elocution
with as little meaning as a blackbird's batty chatter.
So the artist figures things to come, a
        singular discourse.

Longing for meaning can be fixed. First it's a problem,
then it's the cure; but we are dispersed into a rigmarole,
into the telling fishhook of a style, and it
        fluctuates fiercely,

releasing its insights like ink dropped into water.
The audience shivers, watching everything they knew
fracture, their future a lifeless illusion,
        colours dispersing

slowly at first, then faster: their career path diagrams
riddled by lightning. I'm nursing a drink at twilight,
looking up at the thunderheads lit from below:
        everything's blowing

into the future that waits for us but doesn't want us,
nor the children, who await their change of faith,
or so I guess, staring down on the late avenues
        crowded with feelings.

Ariadne on Lesbos

Here the past unfolds in a track of wonder
cramped by black thoughts melting to moonshine: jot down
stuff to notice—sun on the mountains, twilights
    we have enjoyed there,

all delusions crash on the blades, it's strange and
dim. For some, however, it just keeps rolling,
shit and steam and charcoal, to each a holy
    season, a flame-out.

Those who speak up live to regret it: what a
rotten business; then it's a thesis, pewter
glows to silver magically polished as I
    hope to expect you

loving, now this criminal wisdom. Daughters
in their dreams repeat what their anxious mothers
tell them: if they're lucky, they have one chance at
    finding a true love.

Shun the boy's fierce promises, certain heartbreak
follows. Who cares? Amulets tell my future—
jet means sadness, onyx is lucky like a
    delicate kiss, it

rearranges heaven and hell, a heartbeat's
pattern follows, push on the button, slow then
fast; abruptly knowledge and wisdom, cycled.
    Weather and time will

turn the tables. Empty your pockets, see the
sun and moon and zodiac break in pieces,
strew the poison, hack at the blooms that choke the
    garden of childhood.

All that bleak maturity must be cancelled.
On the beach those flashes of phosphorescence:
you will never meet me in clear abandon:
      loosen your syntax.

Yes, it always seems to be part of true love,
how we feed the needs on the lower level.
Leaving things alone is the best, but change is
      better than stasis,

then the sad rehearsal of how we stamp out
trust and honour, duty and tender feelings.
Ah, my crisis beckons, a light that glimmers
      far in the distance.

Now I have my vision: an empty beach. A
bonfire smoulders on the horizon, so that
cruel appraisals hinder and hold a girl back
      from the appointment

fame or fate holds—whatever that is: life, death,
food or light, like water-clock droplets blending
loss with love, it drains me of hope, and then we're
      just about ready.

Something worse than esprit de Boofhead hatches
treason, blocks the traffic of whispered kisses,
so you weep for others, but not their future
      death and destruction.

Hear no evil, never believe those white lies,
buy a fake identity, cheat that god-head,
map the sky. I'll calculate how to offer
      total surrender:

then he'll kiss me under the starlit heavens.
Will he? Blunt the nib that the artist drew with,
faked fantastic angels above us floating,
       dabbled with gold leaf

so their haloes tinkle and flare. The stars gleam
down the arched original path from heaven.
Yes, your voice has travelled a thousand years, and
       winter, withdrawing,

chilled the lips that told us of new betrayals:
gaudy storm-flogged nights with a view of ashen
fields, the high stone palaces burnt and smoking,
       people at hopeless

prayer. The long vowels rose up to heaven, sobbing.
Now my future's foundering, now the clouds clear,
now my Dionysiac grief is just a
       drunk interruption—

past the tangled thickets of lust the night birds
chatter; heaven lightens the sacred discourse
spoken softly: human and goddess, yearning
       sharpens the edge of

eager dream-filled gratification, breathe a
draft of perfume like a declension, now these
heartaches lift me up off the planet, now this
       endless ascension.

Days in the Capital

—after Cavafy

Those coastal fevers are for young people.
They like the heat. Here in the hills

the air's cool. Young love, it takes
your breath away—who can say no?

On a sports field, girls in armour
whack at each other. Evening comes on.

The street lights give out a violet glow.
From time to time you hear a passing car.

I sit up late, reading sad stories
under the light of a lamp called Raymonde.

A Marriage

He takes her hand; she clambers
from the black car and smiles
awkwardly at the crowd of strangers.

Then they push through the audience,
snow or confetti on their shoulders,
equal first to break the tape.

Much later, one either side of the stumbling
baby, holding up the prize by the arms
as they tilt into the glare.

I won't photograph the infidelities;
the housework, the tired afternoons,
the drink, and the scalpelling insults.

He accepts the gold watch and looks for her
among the gathering. Later they wander through
the parking lot, her arm around his shoulder.

The grandchildren are displayed
on the veranda at Resthaven; but
the other guests are watching the TV.

The sun makes a lovely show among the cumulus,
like a painting trying to tell us a story.
A black car idles on the gravel drive.

There's something he wants to say—the words
are on the tip of his tongue. She gives him
that anxious smile, and squeezes his hand.

Falling

The camera lens dips into the river, the silvered
rocks on the bottom—
it's a model, a trick view of rooftops glittering
under a panorama of snow-clouds.
The weather has a pattern—a kind of meaning,
that is. Is it like the meaning of a landscape?
Which is a way of gazing across the plant-smothered
surface of the rickety terrain
from about five feet off the ground, then
you shake it, and the snow begins to swirl?
Ask the designer, who's
a kind of god, she'll know art
from craft, and where politics
threatens our stable view of things.
With a gasp she reaches the sunlight
on the zinc rooftops. Above, a contraption
clattering low over her head.
On the distant horizon a tiny flying machine
glints in the haze, struggling for height.

While we were crunching through the heaps of dry leaves
a new day crept up on us, like that storybook landscape
above the clouds.
                    John
slapped him. Three best friends

The blanket, the picnic hamper unfolded
among the pines—clack!—it sprang open
to answer their wishes. Until that moment
he had not allowed her a safe place in his arms—
her husband said once how she pushes
forward through the rage crowds force on us
through the rapid speech, taller but level-headed
into this surprising middle age, growing younger,

inventing herself, turning and folding back
to a teenage ambience—this is imagined,
but slowly, in the old magazine, and now
it's invading the future, our hot white world:
When you grow, predicts the wise columnist,
your name will be more substantial
than the molecules that make you up—
the car radio, the bracket mounted to catch
the electromagnetic waves—
dithering daydreams—she trudges onward,
now like a child, understanding the subway diagram,
following the directions, always
glowing like a kid drinking a Jolt Cola
in the early winter evening, this inspiration
breathing in the trace of mist above the jacket.
She claims the top echelon, through the moonlight
spooking: the name of the boy's dark cruiser
drifts on silence.

And she turns back from the far shore,
twisting and twinkling in the high afternoon sky
and slowly drifting in the end
towards the brilliant water.

Anyone Home?

I can hear the stop-work whistle
down at the Club, can I go home now?
Then I see Grace Kelly,
        the young Grace Kelly!
'Starlet Fever', that's what it is.
I keep hearing the word 'workaholic'.
Echoing, echoing. The Doc says
        take a tablet.
How do you feel down there? Okay?
Take a dive. Bite the bullet. It's
the jim-jams, I've got the jim-jams.
I think he said 'phenomenology'.
I keep hearing jackhammers, it's
the jackhammers, that's what it is.

Do you know Jacky Rackett?
        Do I know Jacky Rackett?
Lovely type of a feller. Dropped his packet.
I keep hearing syllables, polysyllables.
Do I know Sherelle? Young Sherelle?

Then I hear an Appaloosa, getting closer,
the clip-clop racket in the bracken, then
a clattering gallop on the gravel,
        I hear the hullabaloo.
How d'you do, sir. Jacky Rackett?
Top o'the Paddock, sir, the witch's cat.
Then I can see Grace Kelly again,
up close, it's getting warmer.

Down here in Third Class it's getting warmer.
Pull the toggle. No, blow the whistle.
I keep hearing the word 'histrionic'.
Is that better? Snug in a rug?
          Clacketty-clack.

Do you know Gary Langer? Barry Langer?
They were both practising solicitors.
I keep hearing polysyllables,
          then jackhammers.
Now that's a clavier sonata!
That's the cat's pyjamas! No,
it's the Appaloosa! Barry! Gary!
How are you doing, you old bastard!
I keep hearing these unpredictable
polysyllables, it's like the Name of God.
Isn't God indelible? Indivisible?

I can see a Californian kitchen, I'm
visiting Gidget, isn't she cute?
I can almost reach out and touch her,
gently. I pour us a Coke and it bubbles.
Is this Paradise? Is it really Paradise?

Hey, there's Jack Napier. Jack Napier!
Absolute type of a gentleman. Wouldn't
hurt you with a barge pole. Jack's
a jumper. Jack invented the calculus.
Then I hear a rustling noise,
          highly magnified.
I think I snapped the tape
at the pain threshold, then fell.
Oh Sherelle, will it ever diminish?
Will it ever diminish, and fade away?

Gidget, I'm carrying Gidget, on the beach,
and I stumble! *Bugger it!*

Down at the Club, the Workers' Club,
the stop-work whistle, should I go home now?

I keep hearing 'intelligent,
     very intelligent'.
Push the toggle-button, the green one,
the illuminated one, no, not that,
the other one! You'll feel
worse at first, considerably worse
at first, until the medicine. Oh boy,
some party! Were you there?
     Was I there?
I keep hearing 'medical, paramedical'.
Don't you think it's time to pull the plug?
Push the button? I can see Paul de Man,
Paul de Man, is he in heaven?
I keep hearing 'shoot, parachute'.

Okay, what odds would you give me?
Push the toggle-button, bird-brain.
This one, or that one?
Go home, time to go home.
Quick, put on the Nazi uniform.
He says 'Quick, Sherelle, do as I say!'
Why should I?
     Why should I?
Who do you think I am? He says—
famous Chinese proverbs—he says
'Quick philosopher, dead solicitor!'
Who do you think I am? Paul de Man?

I can hear a whistle, an emergency whistle.
Now I can see the tropical effluent.
I think it's moving in our direction.
Dark stain.
      Dog paddle! Back-pedal!

That's funny, I can't hear a thing.
Ding-dong.
        Anyone home?

The Romans

A sketchy reflection in the smoked window,
less bright than the Roman virtues that
stand around the chair and glare
        back at the glass.

Down in the windy park the leaves all turn
over at the same time—it's the climate
explaining the weather to the workers.
        It's like this:

apart from the isotherms repeating themselves
like a patient discussing with her dentist
composite amalgams and the price of gold,
        there's also change—

mainly decay, the trees explain, waving to
the mail-boys and the minor librarians and
the ibises busy scavenging among
        the lunch wrappers—

it's a helix, looping down into the dark.
I agree, snores the dozing drunk drawing
to the close of his liver's long career.
        From ancient times

to the technical present most things decline;
only the means of oblivion improve. The laughing
gas whispers yes, in Athens and Alexandria things
        were much the same.

Storm over Sydney

Blustering over the Harbour, brilliant rain
slaps and blathers at the rusty Bridge.
I dodge for cover as the sky turns green.
Cars wobble and skid on William Street,
       hot with mechanical rage.

Lightning strikes twice: a blinding white
crack! and the echo whacks the concrete.
I fossick and dawdle in the supermarket aisles
safely underground, among the paper plates
       and the jars of honey.

The thunder has trundled a thousand miles
and boiled the Pacific black to bother us all,
and it's dull and sick from its long journey.
Now I'm trying to wheel a crook trolley
       from the shopping mall:

the chrome's rusty, and a bent wheel clanks.
It's the season of ruby cellophane and holly;
the gutters are chock-full of summer hail
fresh-frozen and smashed into chunks.
       At the café I doze

in a corner, read the messages and the mail,
and unwrap the book I've bought. It's old, old:
the writer's fervour whispering down the years,
epigrams elaborating a narrative—as though
       such fragments could!

On schedule, the weather grumbles and raves
westward over the suburbs. I'm happy. I know
a little park where I can park the car,
sit on a wet bench and watch the waves
       fume in the amethyst air.

Opus Dei

What I have scribbled I have scribbled, and thus
heal and bless, a spooky penicillin quelling a hubbub
of bad blood, thinks the country clergyman.
'Blue Hills' is a frail murmur through static now
and the river heights a warning of how the white man
ruined a continent. He pads through the empty house
clutching a piece of paper, and finds himself in the kitchen
drinking hot chocolate through its gluey skin
and tuning in the ABC at three a.m. on Sunday,
nothing there but an electronic whistle, and fruit bats
       quarrelling in the orchard.

Under the lamp a pale Polaroid explains
how to hold a ball above the surf,
another how to give the dog a bone,
and here's the '39 Buick washed up against the late fifties—
an oil-stained hulk buried in blackberries. He's
halfway through a sermon, ignoring the grinding noises
as history works its gears and gets ready for the steep descent,
       and then the plunge.

What theology endures among the witless, he wonders.
A spiritual headmaster gathers a flock of nods,
a stern father despising the emotions
that will trip him up and bring him down.
So I rant, and offend, laughs the distressed preacher,
why not? It's like burglary—hushed at noon,
the clatter of locks at nightfall—instructing young girls
to tighten up their virtue as an older brother might.
The spiritual talent coach act prospers for a while
then the crowds thin out, frightened
by the rope of spittle swinging on his chin.

Halfway to the city a crush of bright vehicles—
junk mob trouble a freeway bypass doesn't solve—
normally a healthy ruckus, but here malevolent, they
slump at the wheel as the exhaust gas leaks in,
spooling through the urban myths on their way to Heaven—
and no mercy for the timid spirit, warns every chapter.
When he was young, the Good Book got by heart,
no end to his mnemonic tricks—in Salt Lake City,
on Waikiki, the names of Yahweh spilled off his tongue
like a bushel payout from a fruit machine.
The destitute suburbs and the red-dirt farms—
poor, but rich in souls—made up God's fat oyster—
he might as well bamboozle the willing sheep
and strip a wallet a minute, but that's a cheap Yank
ripoff trick, igniting and dousing nerves
in a storm of public tears and a pounding of arteries
halfway from the hospital to the suffocating grave.

From a stalled truck, screaming—fear in the sun—
hillbillies thrashing their brutal young, belt buckle
chopping the scalp, the tongueless howl, but didn't he
expect that? His life seemed like wading into water,
deeper each year, more exhaustion, the storm pushing up
a glut of scum, sluts and bodgies fornicating on the sand,
the grass under the bushes littered with sticky flat balloons.
He rose to his parish in the age of the teen rebel—
the hair Hokusai, the iris delft, narrating himself
from the screen to the gaggle below—among the acolytes,
a surfeit of counterfeits and perversions. How
will our kiddies ever know the touch of the real?

Late at night on the wireless some paid communist
harangues Australia with a theory of church power-greed
feeding off 450-volt paranoia. Projecting fear and hatred

onto a gang of blanks, the pastor grits his teeth—
this is an insult to the Mother of God, and sneering
relegation. He knows all about that—you, chosen; you,
burnt. Good night.
                      Aloof on his windy peninsula,
infusing righteous anger to a tannic brew
he foments anxiety among the young of Balmy Acres,
a ploy from a decade back when good men suffered
brainwashing in Korea for democracy—hullo,
there's also deviation here—rancour, shadows
under the forest canopy, rage boiling over
at the radio preachers raking in the dollars
and the traitor radicals who'd sell us to the Devil—
that riff-raff, their fashion flags (I'm in, you're out)
twisting in the wind among the alien Red Clans.

At the Old Time School Dance the fiend of rectitude
loiters around the dunce stool—childhood!
The bullied and their tardy revenge,
a chill dish, sour in the mouth: invective
in the papers, Letters To The Editor, curses
as cruel as the rogue morality that grunts and reddens
in the poofter's bar; and now in his country town, dozing
at noon, above the bowling green the 'safe-sex' handbills
spin aloft and flutter in the blast of wrath.
Look, they all bear the mark of the Monster,
there's love and hate on each set of knuckles,
kiss and make up; a puncture, then the venom.
And the Country Party? Urbane 'pastoral leaseholders'
or dimwit bumpkins meddling with the truth—
a gaggle of has-been would-be's twirling groggily
into the wee hours on a floor slippery with alcohol.

Down in the City, dealers, bankers and manipulators:
snake-oil salesmen, smart operators who lope aloft
in the big smoke, striding among cloud and rain-wet
rusty steel and glass. You win, but I endure,
sniggers the trendy ripping off the market—his
market, my flock, thinks the shepherd. To shake hands
is a kind of contamination, for that lizard grip
fits yours exactly, and his gelid blood takes
warmth from yours. In despair of water, can the Lord have
planted Capitalism in the wasteland of the human heart?
Lunch at the Church League seems racked with politics—
from mellifluous cadences to the exhibition of stubborn silence
his fellow-soldiers decline and grumble, wondering,
as they watch their sons turn into pimply sin-racked adults
reversing down the drive into traffic accidents or bad marriages,
wondering is it fear or desire that inflicts us
with a burden of memories, or is that a blessing?
All right,
              maybe one drink. Maybe
                            one more.
And so the subtle metropolitan afternoon
simmers with gossip and the fraternal murmuring
of those trusted few—'who could have thought the Beast
had spawned so many? plotting against us,
against our demanding but generous American Friends
and the Lord of Anger.'
                            But in the sight of God those
waves of remembrance flooding up the sand bring us back
from the human swarm and their talent for betrayal
down the shimmering black highway littered with metal
to the gravel roads empty under the sun, the river-flats
rich with resistant pasture species, the kitchen silent
in the cricket-stitch of midday, back to himself,
exhausted, bewildered under apricots and marsupials,

rediscovering lost love in those snapshots
and hope in the washed-out colours, two copies of each print,
our innocent selves brother and sister, the morning light
unstained then, a simple miracle, Christ with white teeth
like the young men, decently dressed, who went out early
bearing black-bound books into the Sunday suburbs—why,

the very standard of living was a Sign—
twenty centuries after the arrest, trial,
torture and execution of a Criminal—copies
of copies as the waves teach us, the rainwater
rising, and darkness under the trees.

North Woods

The whirring projector flings this
onto the screen: she tilts clockwise, leaves
the view of the rocky river flowing out of focus
tangled and white like laundry boiling, slowly
turning her back and moving into the shadow
of the porch, on a cloudy afternoon—the light
tinted pearl, a naked toe bent and dipped
into the water—now she tears herself
from the brilliantly-coloured view and
sweeps into the room—she seems younger,
the hairdo's different, there's less available light here—
like something pushing its way through
        the photo-realist wallpaper—
then she looks into the depths of things, charming
some guests, frightening others—
        what if all our secrets—that's
ill-mannered on this coast, but not on the other.
The old green ferry bumps along through the rapids
and a breeze rearranges the mist so that a rainbow
points down to the earth and the dyes there
are reflected on your trochus shirt button.
The imagination babbles forever,
the kitchen light in the cabin always
glowing in the fog ahead where frail ghosts
glimmered, like a gin ad in the ancient forest,
the sun spoking through the lonesome pines.

Then when she leaves, when she strikes out
into the world, bad things will happen, but
she'll be undaunted, the author insists.
She takes the neon light sparkling on a brooch
        for a sign, and the evening sun

leaking through the clouds and reflecting
on her friend's lips, glinting on the crimson gloss
as she gives a smile—looking up from her typing—

that's right, now I remember—midnight—

in the garden a sunken bowl brimming with rainwater,
reflecting the moonlight—she looks down—*uh!*—then
after waking from the dream she's full of fear,
          her pillow's wet, she's alone,
she thinks about the brain's shabby bargaining,
tangles in the neuron net, the scriptures
in gloomy wolf cover, and the ridiculous promises—
          if she's perfect
she'll live forever, that kind of thing.

Lately my biographer wants me to talk, she says, he's
          fishing for retrospection,
dawdling around in this dead-end shack, then
he skulks back to the city to tell them about it,
the crawlers, so few rise up to the idealistic forms,
each day another friend involved in some
fraudulent racket. In confiding her memories
she assembles a mausoleum,
and she makes inscription and remembrance a cult,
this melancholy scribbling . . . uh huh . . .
counterfeit of intimacy—

There are companies to raid, investments
to be combed and smoothed, patrons to be flattered.

And when she pushes on, when she pounces
on the future, audacious and exemplary,
the authors of her character watch from a distance,
unhappy at what they've brought about.
The sunlight glinting on a coin,
the syrup of happiness filtering to the bottom
of the chill pool where light fails, losing
one wavelength after another, from yellow to blue,
to be preserved there in a kind of memory theatre.

And looking back, the old people weren't real—
that's what they felt; since the kids left home
they'd mutated into an ideal. Then at least
we'll have been made up, they say, a tale
telling us about our sad and radiant feelings,
so we can own them again.

What good is it all, in the end? the children ask.
We're *them*, that's what.
                              She turns—the highlights
on her hair overtaken by shadow—and fades back
into the dim room, and disappears—would we be
satisfied with our childhood, if it happened again?
That's not too distant, as we estimate these things,
not too far away to visit, to lay claim
to our gentlest movements, a forgotten life.

Con's Café

My rage becomes an uproar, but
only in its home, the chest, where
the heart grows jealous of the storms
unfolding there—rage to live, that is,
like a Hollywood painter in a fit
in front of a canvas that won't give up
its treasury of liquid assets, but
finding there a querulous middle age
and a brave array of symptoms
that the street insists on celebrating—
those kids on skateboards and a raft of sun
skidding into Con's Café where the coffee
tells us of its long journey from the mountains
and the hydro-electric schemes our fathers
sweated for—what comic's that you're reading?
Archaeology—the milk-bar mirror's baubled
with cloudy bubbles and scoops of light—
and the first-year girls in cardigans
are almost 'sophomores', but only in the light
reflected from a distant movie screen—

outside, the twilight, and a College Ball, boys grooming themselves
like a rank of violinists, and soon with their partners making up a
pack of matched doubles practising their roles—to govern us, the
dance insists—join, then divide—outside in the private College
garden it's a harvest moon, you can hear the limousines purring on
the gravel drive, the mothers are grinning over the hedge in fur
coats, sorrowing for the loss of their daughters, but then, an accrual
of assets falling into place under the dim portraits, the features the
painter struggles to get just right—true, but not too true, kind,
but interesting—interesting, that is, in the investment sense of the
term.

At Naxos

I write to you from the end of the world.
Long ago the others disappeared
over the lock bridge across the canal,
then through the gorge and into the caves,
down through the cellars, past
the dusty bottles of wine, under the trapdoor,
down the greasy wooden steps, and
into the dark caverns where you can hear
the sea rumbling and sucking far away,
then down the steps cut into the stone, then
further down into the earth.
I chose the sunlight.
Yes, it is lonely: a pale ribbon in my hand,
leading to water, tunnels under the water,
railways under the sea, rhythmic noises
designed to please fish, and glints of light—
blue and green, with lemon and gold at the edges
like a fringe—that seem to fall down and down,
twisting slowly, reflections from the sandy bed
that rise up, that float up to the surface

where the sun flatters the ocean with glitter and distant machines
plough the waves endlessly, plough and sow the waves through the
summer season, and in winter—winter that is already upon us, so
quickly—in winter they harvest the skeins of low grey cloud, almost
a mist, distilling rain, in the lower left-hand corner of the picture
a fine rain that anoints the canal machinery.

Two Views of Lake Placid

Here at last in Holiday-Land—click!—I'll
just pull the jeep in to the kerb and
pick up a few drenched senior folk—
damp complaints as we idle down the avenue—
pines dripping in the fog, then it's
chit-chat time, around the camp-fire.
A candour invaded the trailer park like
nerve gas and fastened onto scenes projected
wavering on the polished side of an Airstream—
so many tender imaginations adrift
in an atlas of pain some lesser recording angel
forgot—what subject for pilfered emotions,
compiled in a quick slither of slides—hey,
where are the kids? how they turn, half-
lost in the summer glare and say goodbye, that
skimpy peck, a lilt of the heart and they're
gone, I'm a kindness glutton in a love swindle—
ship me back to Korea 1953 cadence candid
dance refrain, body-bags abolish
crimp ingot pursuit jacket

abreast of that authority a scarce crop a leeway truth spouse grew
to be a permanent frail guide the worker grapevine whirling with
gossip, arms-control study out of control on Route Nil, a cycle of
pillage then reimbursement bare henpeck, as pluck plunge over-
eater in a racket vacation jaunt becoming wobbly—he drinks too
much now, I guess he can't drive accurately—artless wind-up, quick
flimsy trot—how long?—cancel

Snap

A rainbow, tinted various pale shades—the
green and light brown seem made for each other—
curves over the shoulder where leaves whisper
and arches into a background of grain and shadow,
more the effect of the half-smile than anger
or the addiction to rapid speech, or so we think.
The subtle check fabric of the shirt speaks of
a cultural niche to do with class and brand-names,
then the words that shuffle out across
the horizontal pages claim large areas
of sensual experience and pain thoroughly studied
as if by divine right, lit by a glow from
the top of the frame above where the house pets
and the badgers begin to quarrel, either
the lurid cumulus in the sky or a kind of spotlight
elevated above the drive-in corral of emotions.
There, the voice says gently, every fact is being
added up, each colour assigned to bold or pastel,
and now here's the postman with something surprising
for you to sign. Make up your mind.

Now escape if you can, for all this is locked into the past, and has
become repetitive and irreversible. In the morning light that you
are so grateful for you read the paper, absorbed like a child in the
tinsel advertisements and busily unravelling the dramas that weave
their plots in the suburbs—but if you looked up, you'd see yourself
seated in a café in a European town that seems to have moved
back to 1934 or thereabouts, while a young woman—your mother—
is moving slowly about the room, lighting the lamps, one by one, as
evening falls.

Old Europe

Turn from these old men sobbing on the sand;
turn from the waves, their iodine-perfumed shocks.
In that bowl of hot silence behind the dunes
recall the way their lives rose up to havoc
and prayer; and then we hear the visiting angels
rustle down the towpath to the bridge.
At noon, a young man slumbers under the hedge,
dreaming in its thick, unspeaking shade.
Through the afternoon they watch the sun
sail over France, and beneath the fiery sky
engines roaring, and the sound of tank-treads
clattering beyond the shoulder of the road:
they slump in the heat, sick with fatigue,
the eyeball dazed with rapid glimpses,
a blaze of fetid light, shook foil shining
on the mirror of the flooded field. Blackbird,
dart out from the shattered window,
cease your psychic striving, with your
blue-black feather and your orange eye:
in the whirling murmur of your chatter

how frivolous this frightened youth appears, grunting and bursting
with energy on the attack and then soaked with wild tears after-
wards, hearing his own memories creep and stumble from one
wounded denial to another. He'll end up sobbing in some veter-
ans' home, slumped on a mattress, his scented spark of life quite
quenched. Now the goddess Europa descends on the wrecked and
smoking town, and heaps up the abandoned square with cobalt-
coloured grapes and purple figs. See her roam the cool weed-
covered bank with shreds of sun caught in her hair.

Box Contaminant

To claim a fault so arrogant, you queer,
the old school tie, the memory slip, their
acid drop of jeering's hardly evidence, this
group stare of dead fellows full of grog severity,
no, no adventure for the oral gimmick such torment,
no flagrant blueprint, this simple dominant stamp
proof of right to bully, so what, at this distance?
Tooth fairy dent dexterity from opposite tent intimacy
are these definitive folk, these rich corrupted folk,
what precise claims so thirsty they dare call a snap?
And so to their stingy promises, so what, who are you?
Their cool promiscuous biting, your own future slack
cracked fantasy—can you validate your stripped vision
properly in the bauble grove—Hey, Chubby Brother,
you new kids beat up a proper clash, now drum up
the wintry fairies and their magic curses
to the birch tromp dance I truly toil and settle
in my rhythms at some stage prior to the enigmatic
sunken treasure, my flight path rich kids sonata
proof of richer fathers and their English doom

and their pout and their cosy theology, furthermore this God
pampers class apparatus woollen gown and the burning cigar may
well mush up this bloody myth in the jumbo fictitious amuse-
ment—why transcendental? Why not? It's no simple ruse to study
scuttled the layover top-drawer plagiarism the reign keels over to
fritter and chew out buckle passionless memorial poke, no climax
prick, no reticent cryptic orthodox dark agony hurting more than
bearable and remember this

A Plume of Ash

When the medication hits, the freeway appears to
curve and wobble, and at the end a building
full of lunatics: work your way through the wards
inscribing their ramblings and the letters
they want to write, but can't—begging
and cursing, some thick with legal threat—
using pink and ashen ink, colouring in
these reveries of a fresh start,
how she pressed the knob by the screen
and everything started all over again,
the mistakes and the accidents, for which
she was to blame, running backwards
into the future, all that.
Beyond her reach of memory the horsemen
gather together, or just plain late
the escapade goes on blabbing, and
dipped and wrinkled in the pool it seems
the moon dwindles above a soldier's bald head,
double disk, and as glib as a Martian poet
floods the garden with tinsel.

She sinks back in the chair, the telephone cold and dead in her
hand, as though she's had enough of this sexual activity, the stories
gushing like a stream of dirty water, and guilt an emetic spasm.
Breakfast makes an unhappy frame for my stories—let's look at
the Third Person: weaving down the highway he's too late in this
cold spring weather, his tale is over. But if he lives long enough he'll
see the spectre of the sun glowing on an overcast afternoon, the
rose-gold light fiery on the crusted snow.

Chicken Shack

By the second reel you're exhausted;
pull onto the gravel. In the shadow of the hut
twin girls. Lax in the luminous sunset,
fervid later, in the Ektachrome track
of your voyage, that melancholy fable,
your lust for food and drink becomes
their lustrous knack for franchise marketing—
now the bartender's dabbling with his hobby,
some hydraulic bric-à-brac, doodling among
fountains and waterfalls of tumbling crystal.
Across the dirt track, above the wet foliage:
is that mesmerising purple cloud mountain
the concoction of two Bayou Pepper Vodkas
too many, or is it me? The 1930s wallpaper,
redneck radio and its feverish
contempt—now cop frolic—new car,
newer than ours—and what he wears
on his hip demolishes their poor
white trash birthright, such as it is:
free speech, First Amendment, and so forth . . .

Now the halftone twinkle and the print glitch drift down on our
consumers from the overhead grate, now she says put up your
bright weapons lest the dew rust them, no more rock'n'roll in this
backwater. Her sad marriage trinkets glitter on the carpet; in this
arena pensive daydreams grow and glow through magazines and
the TV shopping channel to breakfast promise and abandon,
though heedless of its future, a mist obscuring memory, lawfulness
slowly solidifying out of anarchy—my need is to separate the vivid
families who dwell in danger of capitalism run amok, faith turned
agnostic, from those whose politics is simply a pale panic. Just regis-
ter, you don't have to vote. No way, no say. Not this chicken.

Cable Chimp

The old man needs a whisky at the academic
roadblock and they give him coffee powder,
hot water from a tap, and sugar cubes—
is he an old nag, to nuzzle thus?—all this
in a truncated cone of polystyrene.
Here the happy hoop-jumpers rank him
or his good works as a minor flash
in a public socket while behind the curtain
a mechanic uncouples the slot machine funnel;
then pleasantly postmodern comes the bluff and
counter-bluff; now the tease, now the feint,
the boob-tube factor waffling in the rear.
Now they're all fondling the culture tokens,
now this discourse bundle is a rapture cult
among undergrads; I guess it's time for him
to 'fess up to a secret authorial intention,
some hankering to rig a covert climax, plot-wise,
and a fleeting desire to flee robot sex—
text couplings—and go look for the real thing,
and here's the vice Chancellor, batting her lashes:

I was a harlot, searching for an alien harmony—oh abundant miss,
the hack responds—inscribe our intertwining as a twinkling spiral,
a stealth kiss fuck underlined by a nib's tracery, and oh the spirits—
here a nook, there a cranny, now a jealous shot, then a deadbolt,
now a clouded riddle tumbling down to the lower heaven—in the
wreck ardent passion glue doctoring a clique of peppy brilliance,
and the desire that rotates our ages from youth to silliness brings
us now to stamp out deadlock menace, erase that teen shroud of
lust and canary silk schooling—we are the lost lookout and the
forlorn band.

Bells Under Water

On safari, sport and booty,
a widow hoists the leash
the tellers chuckling
now they take over Tinseltown:
the jumbo painkiller plazas,
those hustlers dog my step and that
spicy dusk gusting—I laze under
the banyan on a banana lounge and
watch the mascot of some fabulous
bygone coterie wink and wobble
then plunge into a lack of talent.
Herewards ambles Amber, warlike flirt,
with mismatched woozy codger:
id est, Hubby Snookums
in pursuit, last night's boozy
breach amnesed. Now twilight, a smoky
flavour, pillages my heart then theirs,
old sots: their grizzling needs
direct them to theft, then theft again,
faking those heartfelt memories.

O Big Smoke, render winter, back to the thirties where I live, lived,
now gone under, tram symphony why so dominant, you coddler,
those night-clubs, your joke trombone why so psychological? It's no
big trick playing tootsie, but how to keep it up, the dreams bigger
than any art, the heartbreak more brutal than a laurel wreath in its
withering, then the decade collapses into shit and thunder—your
watery grave awaits no bribe availeth slide under glass-green deep
good night

Aurora

I love the radiance of the Reached Zenith,
but there's also a swerve to remember—
the junior glow, the teen fracas, drifting
among skittish louts and kids
malingering behind the snack frames—
siblings hiding in a heap of theology, that
locker. Jab and gargle, Drain-Brain,
make a zig-zag run for the future!
Patrol—window choked with tourists—
that lolls past the floral clock, and
idles by the turkey-talkers watching
a sundial doze in the shade of a tree.
Nightfall—the cruise grumblers, called 'Jumbo'
and 'Drop-Kick', snooze; in a back paddock
the starlight jalopy dump breeds dreams.
Dumb in the pokey this small town admits it is,
the sleepers wander in the fields of childhood;
ah, bright graduation: it's the
turncoat kid giving the farm away
for Sin City, burning the vacant role

Just as you're strutting in the avenue vocal with juveniles, it forms
a dreadful pattern—don't you merit a hi after all those cycles? And
time avenging, in the village pub a line-up of slender singles groggy
in the purple light, the hoon range brute drudge-drivers, why, auto-
matic Country & Western, this is the monochrome fifties your heart
a banging pump, the old bus grinding gears pulling out in rain-
swept daybreak, grey paint smeared and winter overcoat decorum
exit our hope gap bye-bye lacklustre muddy chief route abyss

From *Different Hands* 1998

Neuromancing Miss Stein

Hemingway looked in to see the great artist he really was, or could be if he tried hard, and instead found Janet Scudder and the Famous Writer there at the zinc bar at the front of the café, talking and drinking cassis. Miss Stein had a little book with her, something we all ought to know about, but to know it too thoroughly would be a mistake. Janet was a little removed from herself, that is, from her own problems, per medium of cassis and white wine, and the transatlantic mail. Janet said that Hemingway wrote with color and energy whole paragraphs that simply meant shit. His eyes reminded her of Minnesota, and of the things that could be seen in Minnesota. She was also reminded of sheep going to slaughter, and of her wish that Americans would leave America and then go back again.

Those women, they were both awfully busy and wanting. Then they met Jean Cocteau, who prided himself on his pride, and they invited him to a dinner at the Café du Commerce. He wore a bright yellow tie and a dark grey jacket, and drank three bourbons rather quickly and then said in front of the company 'The prize has to go to the one, you know, the one to pass Hemingway first, because he is not liked by many.' For the American writer, such a comment was a kind of Parisian imprimatur. He said that, ah now, naked. His teeth bared. And there in front, a woman in a trench-coat. Her throat excited.

Well-liked or not, Hemingway's career started at that point and moved sideways, instinctively getting these experiments to go with the pulse of the French cultural electrodes, and though it might seem that he had little in common with Miss Stein, he could talk to painters and people like that, and he was interested in the technicalities of writing.

The restlessness of his work, the madly swirling shades of Hemingway, that was nothing. Gertrude Stein was interested in what was in his head. For his part, he was fascinated by the enormous flocks of Gertrude Steins we had surged out from lunch to see, sailing above the city. We looked up, but they had the advantage: they looked down on Paris. Only a rectilinear chamber in a seamless universe of pacts would get rid of those thousands of eyes.

He said 'Up there, above Europe, she invented modern writing—but epidemics of ambiguity also, and she was not yet supreme creator of the mistral. She was on the verge of that, then she gave it up.' He was speaking in enthusiastic flanges, of course, and he would kiss your ass, in case he decided it should be whipped.

That Hemingway, writing with his twelve sharpened pencils—always like a crab, kind of crooked. At the Commerce he did not come to the tables where we ate, but he noticed Miss Stein's yellow silk hat and he shouted from across the bar 'Words are wordy, and silk is silken; that's it!'

She said 'Hemingway, he thinks he's the next number. He says he knows it. So much he knows, he knows nothing. He wrote lots of sentences, but I do not call them literature,' said Miss Stein, 'as will be obvious to those who read my words.'

'Always in Paris,' said Janet, 'the human traffic is interested in fame and also in indifference to fame, which is why T. S. Eliot said "Gertrude Stein, you were a great admired eldrich that evening in the dark. You were." And it's true—your lists are remarkable.'

'To be an eldritch and to get lists of people is easy,' she said, 'but to get lots of friends is different. For example, my dear Janet, you must remember to say you like Hemingway's work, the three poems and the little song he sang for us the other day, no comment, no argument, and you must take care not to forget.'

The girls began to lick the catch of the gold Dunhill. We were twenty-six at table—some dinner. Kate's bust was sheathed in platinum and cloisonné. One of the smart young artists at the back bar asked 'Miss Kate, why on earth would you induce such a vibrant line in such an enclosed space?' His hair was smoothed back and seemed to be printed on his skull. Janet wanted to hit him, but we pulled her off.

So we decide to go for a walk together, Miss Stein and I. I began to see a meaning in good food. It was printed on a card in front of the restaurant at Passy; the owner had signed off for the winter. *Remember, mademoiselle,* the card said, *the café has moved.* We arrived at the café in a nylon harness that time. Along the Seine, the police raised the foam barricades again.

The mother of the Spanish painter Picasso lived on top of a building then; we ended up going there. Hem said he would be interested in travelling up in the elevator if Janet would, and she was on the red side of paradise, she said, meaning she had been drinking from the little bottle in her handbag, so we had fun going up to the old lady's. Hemingway took out an indelible pencil and licked it and copied a lot of little poems on the inside of the elevator door and—bingo!—there we were.

The poems got him excited, and he was thrashing about, so we all held him as the elevator arrived. *There it is!* he said, pointing at the window. He had suffered a flashback, a vision of the sky that arched over the war, all smoke and shrapnel.

'Why Gertrude Stein chose to say that the war was a nice war,' Virgil Thomson said, 'Captain Hemingway has never understood, and she should not have said that.' Virgil was always checking into her writing, and always very preoccupied. 'They were all sick of her capital capital capitals,' he added. 'Spelling, grammar, syntax—it's enough to drive you mad.'

Finally all they talked about was split infinitives, how it is best to firmly split them, and the icebreaker as a kind of blank space in the chatter, a buffer zone before the real talk, for example: 'We don't exist by ourselves, and our art doesn't exist by itself, but it helps if we think it does, to pervert the subjunctive, and then it consists in what we thought while we were at Saint-Remy.'

Ezra Pound had finished his business with what he called the great literary vagina of London, and now he had come to Saint-Remy to visit, and all we had to offer was Hemingway and rather poor prose. I remember seeing a great bitterness in his manner, though he smiled constantly, in a nervous way. Ezra was always against what he called the 'Old Concentral Bank', and with the drop in currency he suffered a tattooed lozenge of visits, in the bed.

Janet Scudder said 'This Ezra, he thinks he is a big deal, as big as the Mississippi River. Not so. About as big as your average *pissotière* would be about right.'

'You Americans, you are *les incompréhensibles* whom Picasso's mother-fucker objected to,' Cocteau said, his American slang as confused as his clothes. 'You crowd us out, with your lack of talent. It was permanent Americans in Paris wall to wall, that's what it was, and then a punch in the ribs to wake them up.'

'Ah, but to work here in Paris,' Janet said, 'so much more energy than Pittsburg, than Oakland smouldering black smoke across the Bay.' She was always praising Paris, her throaty voice marvelling at this and that.

Miss Stein said of Cocteau's taste: 'His good taste has been approved, primarily, by himself. He would as soon write his own reviews and have them printed in verse in a friend's magazine. Janet was different. Janet I had printed later, dear Janet who had an old camera wrapped in Spanish bull-fighting cloaks in my apartment.'

Hem and Miss Stein went to see a young French painter at Nice who attracted them by the smart way he operated. 'Grant us young people the ability to keep up with the more difficult Americans,' the painter said.

'Oh,' said Gertrude Stein, heavy with demons.

She and the painter got on perfectly: she was a head, nothing more, and he was a brush, and that was enough.

'Art is a gamble,' he said.

Gamble? She thought of lots of people going in to the casinos along the front, among turquoise rectangles and the fine salt spray, to the routine of their games and gadgets. 'I never wished for such things when I lived in California,' she said. 'Do it, use the grammar of gambling games for your art if you want, but do it poetically.'

In the casino, a young man was standing before an illuminated screen. It was pulsing and shivering, throwing out tiny waves of light on grammatically correct planes. 'A pulsing doesn't matter,' Miss Stein said to him, 'especially a literary pulsing, but an art that uses pulsing can be hard to understand. The relief to me of seeing the article that explained the pulsing can never be explained,' she added. 'My work is built on that.'

Hemingway said later 'She would begin with the sentences, the paragraphs, the vocabulary et cetera, which were there all along, among the common people. It was the way she processed it that made her seem a second Godiva. Everybody's anxiety focused on her. She looked at the procedure of writing, and conceived of many things to annoy the bourgeoisie, in case they thought her books beautiful instead of interesting. *Growl and scratch them,* she was fond of saying.'

On a holiday in Portugal, Gertrude Stein had hopes that her automatic writing might trigger avalanches of donkeys and other animals down the rocky street. Now that would be writing to make your eyes pop out! Think of it, spinning out, sub-programs whirling in shades of new yen from the center of Gertrude Stein, it's really too fantastic!

'There's no soul in that,' Mr Eliot said. 'It's not deep enough.' But though he had a little Sanskrit, he was no intellectual; he was more like a salesman who has made a practice of thinking through a dozen impossible theorems every morning, and so exercised his brain. A brain isn't a soul, that much is obvious.

T. S. Eliot did these brain exercises, like thinking up anagrams for the rhetorical term *litotes,* his pale eyes as blank as two plates of vichyssoise. Someone said he 'dressed like a cadaver to conquer Europe,' not like a poet. 'Speak to me,' he would say, 'of control panels and the Episcopalian religion, and give me the magic word.'

Fat chance, she would reply.

Eliot thought her friend Muriel Draper's work was loose, 'Hanging loose like drapery,' he'd say, and chuckle. And he said that her drapery was like some loony contribution to a nisei surgical boutique. So they talked on the terrace, arguing in a friendly way, and—without fully realising it—creating modern literature, or at least creating a small though important regional segment of it. The Riviera leaned into the spring wind for the making of amiability.

Then he discovered that she had a woman in her bed now, naked on a trip and he said, *comme vous êtes méchante.* Janet's black flower lay at their feet, and they both felt the force that raged behind her and spun out, sub-programs whirling like a broom.

Hemingway said 'You know my wife told Gertrude Stein she liked the first thing she ever saw of hers, and she knew she was being tremendously unreliable. My first wife, that is. Everybody talked about that new kind of writing, how the old writing was gone now, at this point. And where was the new stuff, really? Up in the loft with the possums. C'mon, sister. We're best forgotten,' he said. 'The twentieth century can do without us.'

I knew Miss Stein well in those days, though she pretended we had hardly met. The keen students came and asked us what had happened here, in the old days in France, but we were tired, we moved slightly and we were written about and books were printed. So the century groaned and ground on. 'Were you guys illuminated,' the students asked, 'or just switched on?' Miss Stein sniffed, and stalked off in the direction of the canal.

Hemingway scowled at the white duck jacket Miss Stein wore as she walked across the image of the meadow, and tried to disconnect his thoughts. 'That's what's going to happen,' he said, 'people asking stupid questions, decade after decade, to the end of time.'

The Howling Twins

The twins Marilyn and Stanley and their friend Charlie Rugg had stopped at the top of the hill, propped against their red bikes. They'd come rocking along to the farm at Rockaway Junction to see if they could find their pet cat named Snowball. Snowball had been rescued from Uncle Daniel's farm a dozen times, but no permanent good had ever come of it. They'd looked and looked, to no avail.

'Well, I guess Snowball has given us the cold shoulder again,' Marilyn said. 'She hid in her own kitty heaven, a heaven in the underbrush. She would have heard a dog barking, should a dog have barked. Hey, don't you two want me to pick some apples while I'm here? I'm hungry. Maybe she'll turn up, while we're waiting. Maybe somebody has already found the little tyke.'

'Sure, and maybe a bunch of guys grabbed the critter, and took her as sacrifice to their dreadful god Moloch,' Charlie replied scornfully, 'guys who had seen Snowball but who said nothing, nothing at all!' He burst into tears. Marilyn comforted the poor fellow, who was now dreaming of the breasts of the boys, sobbing after they had been crushed by the stone god.

In the quiet country morning there were sounds of many animals. Stanley's acute hearing trapped the other sounds, and sorted out their pet's bickering meow. 'Cats hear more than we know. I hear one meowing now, up in the branches.'

'Uh-uh. I don't see a cat rescued from the branches,' Marilyn said. 'Not by us, at any rate.'

It was fun at Uncle Daniel's farm, but that was a vacation, not employment, which is each day suffering money burning in wastebaskets. The one symbolic escape is amnesia, and the only escapees are those who watch from the place of forgetfulness.

Marilyn listened to the spiritual sounds on the old metaphysical telephone. Lots of static. Then Death spoke, and said he was coming to get the boys. What was their crime? It was looking upon Death himself. How to escape him? Look upon Life.

'To look upon Life,' Marilyn said, 'we could visit dives in the city and from the anonymous dark watch the incomprehensible jazz criminals perform with their flow of semen, or so Charlie once proposed. If I felt like it I could accuse Charlie of something awful, something to do with his body.'

'Marilyn, I'm sure you would accuse the stoops off a building if you could,' snapped Charlie, who had overheard. 'I don't give a damn if you worry about my body. I don't know what to do next with this body, which is more than I can say for you. I've been places, remember.'

Marilyn remembered Charlie had gone to find out what was happening on the West Coast, and Stanley had claimed to be the True Consciousness and said he didn't need to go there to find out. But he did go, and he found there the three old shrews: the stunned governments of capital, insulin and electricity.

Stanley, who wept for the boys the starry-spangled shocks of harlequin speech had led astray, Stanley, climbing the stairways of sin in empty lots, Stanley who jumped into the void of insulin, Stanley who lounged hungry and speechless and said 'Kiss the ass of war, the monster whose fingers inscribe the terror.' Stanley, who is still cursing at the harpies of the poem of life, burning a light in his naked room as a shrine. Stanley thought of Cocks and their monstrous Bombs. In the evening sky, the two twins were visions.

In his dream Stanley finds Snowball and flings the last radio of hypnotism into the East River.

Charlie fondled Marilyn. 'I love you,' he said, insincerely.

'I do too,' said Marilyn. 'Switch that light on, will you, Stanley?'

'As the godhead illuminates itself,' Stanley said, flicking the switch, 'so imaginary walls collapse, and the skinny Legions rush outside to be sick. What you are, you are, that's the wisdom. The ghostly boys build harpsichords in jail, and the players are waiting when an angel's voice calls out *Boys, stop that!*'

Charlie said that Stanley was turning into someone weird and wiggy, and said that a wig of blood is like a debt always running up.

'You never repay that debt,' he said. 'Back in sixty-eight you twins were wiggy, and we were expelled from San Francisco, the city known as the lower realm of demons. There were innocent kids in the street asking for their shoes to be filled with free steam heat.'

'That's tragic,' Marilyn said. 'No one gets shoes full of steam heat. Not in America.'

Charlie recalled Snowball's epiphany: 'Snowball was so high in the estimation of the angels that the Heavenly Hospital illuminated her hair like electric snow. Can you imagine that? Are you jealous?'

'Yes,' Marilyn cried out. 'I can well imagine that! A lost angel! Oh, Mother, I'm with you in Rockland! Where fifteen or twenty miles along the highway a shuddering winter midnight glows, and off in the Bronx I'm shaking with shame, rejected yet confessing, but prepared to go out whoring with the machinery of this invisible madman. Let me pay for luncheon at a restaurant, let me record the final doom of the machinery of Moloch whose loveless tasks and Peoria bone-grindings show us the last sad light flashing above the parks! Moloch, whose soul rushes out from its body, whose robot apartments expelled from their pilgrimage a little sister— what shall we do?'

No one knew exactly what to do next.

Then Charlie's bleeding hand, where Snowball had scratched him, showed a sign. They had looked long enough for forgotten animals. Charlie had already found Snowball, and then lost her again. Charlie had moved Moloch's stone heart to beat, whose skyscrapers crush pederasty, and what good came of it? The sign writhed and pointed to the west.

Charlie felt he had to explain. 'It's like trying to understand the Chinaman of Oklahoma discoursing on the rhythm of the cross-country jazz jam, seventy hours into the woods and the music just beginning, the rhythm still clicking. You try, you get somewhere, and then nothing happens. This means, go west. That's all it means.'

Fine, but where to find salvation? Ask the angels who wander around Uncle Daniel's farm in the fever of spring, ask them where the forgotten animals disappear, follow them through the iron dreams of backyards and movie houses' rickety rows, follow on from Bellevue to Museum to the Hudson under those heaving genitals, past demonic industries scattering bleak phonograph records of time, those angels with their holy yells who float off the ground and fall into the lake, angels red-eyed and angry.

Uncle Daniel's friend the Brilliant Spaniard asked if he could come around, and brought a catch of sardines wrapped in a clean handkerchief, and a draft of his forgotten novel stained with animal soup.

The theme of the novel was the need to escape the horrors of the mundane world, and it made Uncle Daniel think. 'I'll tell you what, old Dago pal,' he said. 'Let's put an advertisement in the paper, enquiring after the secret of illumination. As soon as we see who answers, and it's bound to be the FBI, we'll go straight to Mexico, leaving no indication of where we've gone. They'll never find us there. Unless we go broke,' Uncle Daniel added.

'May the Heavenly Twins forfend,' said the Spaniard, and crossed himself.

'There in Oaxaca the archangel of Third Avenue dreams his iron dreams,' said Uncle Daniel, his voice rising, 'with a flush of remorse, confessing out of the branches. There we'll be in the streets of sorrows, praying to the same archangel in the shadow of dungarees and undressing by his shrine as the wind bothers the trees.'

The Spaniard spoke. 'You and I, we should open a store,' was his opinion.

So Uncle Daniel decided to open an antique store in Mexico and they went, leaving tears and sobbings, joyfully hearing over their shoulders the twins calling them to come back.

'To find what we need to find,' Stanley said, 'it's time to drive!' and in the blowing wind the twins and their pal were pursued by madness, starting in fear as each bough crashed on the roof, aiming for Denver—offering joy to the fleeting time, yet putting down roots.

A glimpse of small-town ecstasy: out back of the roadside diner, in the dusky parking lot, a lonely petticoat fluttered.

'Petticoats,' said Stanley, his hands guiding the wheel. 'Of the goddess Isis, fond of many petticoats, it is reported that her heroes were only driven mad when sudden Manhattan struck them, and then they sat through the tales of the children to hear the holy name in the sure and certain hope of being healed, for it is said that children unknowing have that gift.' So Stanley said to Charlie. 'Nobody can leave my little sister when she speaks, when she prophesies with flashes of genius. She entrances them, Manhattan strikes them, and they know nothing more. The people there, they say petticoats, they say breasts, until they grow dizzy. Their conversation is destroyed by unbearable flashes of consciousness.'

They stopped at a diner, and as soon as soup was served Stanley's sister cried out in a fit of prophecy, excited now she was lost in this new experience, a vision of a dozen naked angels eating lunch with glowing pacifist eyes, enduring hallucinations and then running outside.

'What is Manhattan but a catalogue,' she said, 'a variable measure of poor human prose and immortal verbs? As a city it shouldered its own despair, as an idea it crawled out from under the fashions and flavours of the fifties. The madmen of Los Alamos wailed, who ate fire in paradise alleys aiming for New York, the whole boatload of lost animals.' She recognised something in the style of that hallucination, and at once thought of Mr Bobbsey. She quickly checked, and sure enough, he did it.

'I did that hallucinating,' he admitted, reaching for Marilyn's breast. 'I did it for you.'

'We'd better go home, don't you think, dear?' Mrs Bobbsey asked. Charlie said yes, they'd better.

'You guys are certainly smart,' Marilyn said, when the adults had gone. 'Why, I once caught Mr Bobbsey doing things he shouldn't do. We twins, we had been driving cross-country seventy hours from Denver. To keep awake we mixed dexedrine and hot spirits with orange juice and chilli peppers. That was nothing. Once we crossed the continent without a break, methedrine sodas our salvation. Everywhere, suburban tracts like lobotomies.'

'Aw, you'd think only junkies have feelings,' Charlie said. Charlie owned shares in a condo in Malibu.

'All losers have feelings,' shrieked Marilyn. 'The boys and girls in empty lots, kids with sparkling eyes and intelligent brains, losers who drank nitroglycerine and whacked their heads against the wall! You think they don't have feelings?'

'Oh, give it a break,' said Charlie.

Lost on the Jersey Turnpike the boys came unto Manhattan again, among stumbling pedestrians in tatters. Marilyn jumped up and down in their minds: new loves of a mad generation lying down on the ground at midnight by the highway and staring up at the constellations, their philosophy a hunch welded to a list of saints. They didn't think then of boys sobbing because of their lobotomy, boys who now watch the lawn grow the poisonous grass of capitalism and are paid to mow it, boys who drove trucks into the river and who drove the black locomotive to Harvard laughing.

'Well, no response from the academies for the epiphanies and despairs of ten years' freakouts and root beer insights,' Charlie Rugg complained.

'Maybe we brought them down, with our bad poetry,' Stanley said.

There was a timid knock on the door. 'Don't tell me, it's Uncle Daniel back from Mexico, isn't it?' Charlie said to himself. He was disgusted by now. Uncle Daniel, who hiccupped endless hooch and bop eternity outside the highway diner, who collapsed and went to jail. There are great suicide minds in jail, but just as many loonies.

But it wasn't Uncle Daniel, it was the twins coming home from the hunt for Snowball, bleak with despair.

Then they found the basket in the laundry. In the basket was the cat. Charlie gaped at the beast. 'Motionless in Moloch,' he said, 'the cat whose fate ran through my dreams and so I stumbled and sobbed all night! I shall build it a monument, I shall make it into something magnificent.'

They linked hands, the power kicked and flowed between them, and it seemed they were walking in the streets of love, where dream spirits read the stanzas of their brains and visionary angels crazy in the public parks shouted their fond agreement to the end of time.

From *Gasoline Kisses* 1997

The Duck Abandons Hollywood

I flew my long uphill glide to immortality
solo, on flammable celluloid. O idle frenzy,
stockpiling cans of cartoons—and what splashy
comeback glitters next week? *Fat chance!*—
this taunt from a gaggle of my dusky betters
dabbling around the lagoon—better? because
more 'natural'! My siblings babbling scuttlebutt—
me, guilty? of what betrayal? Human gestures
dignify my tribe, those phantoms in the chalky beam
heal while they gyp and flim-flam. Past tense!—
yes, radical as any Method stratagem, my hackery
deified suburban angst, bum gigs, tantrums.
Steering thus through fits and suffering,
I grew complex—a troubadour could not but be
bisexual, I reckon, in such a wiggle rig. Vain
fakery, stars mutter, swapping their knacks
back and forth amid the smoke and buzz in Lindy's.
I'm still chipper—no, those soul-sisters flapped
and cackled in my bad dream; they damned me, then
gulped their bubbly gush, and giggled—puzzling mirth . . .

I'm a chronic dope, sure thing, fondling this enigmatic image—
oh, whacked out in my den I drivel, in spent or flaky vein. Up there
my horrid flocks disrobe upon that indifferent retina which is the
paradise of quarantine—what's each verbal mouthful worth, what
are dreams patched up from—water-colours in a box? And when I
tally up what booty this greed for godhood got me—*numbers flicker,
blank screen*—my feathered bulk chokes on misery, and nods off with
the spirits—mayhap in our 3-D Cinerama Hunting-Ground we'll
reminisce and chortle—crystal spirits in a jug of hooch.

From *Blackout* 2000

Blackout

Thunder heard—speak to ourselves,
play the men. Hear him?
Assist the counsellor; use your authority;
make yourself ready
                    I say.
Miserable howling!
I felt justified in experimenting.
We are less afraid
as leaky
            her two wet mouths
Paradise-blue baboon lusts
merely cheated
my wife.

§

Wild stinking fire, love and death
in the golden land. Brave cry;
master of meddle pluck my eyes;
hair inquisition, concluding 'Stay.'
Obey five women in the dark power—
a little mirror.
No worse, foul girl; manage my liberal arts,
a stencilled white number;
study the government secret studies,
how to trash new creatures, officer.
They're not prisoners. What tune
hid my trunk? My mind
all popular, my false revenue,
my memory, indeed, would cure deafness.

To have no needs . . .
                    dry annual stooping.

Mark his brother.
He has just hooked down five dexedrines.

My grandmother—good enemy—
was treacherous one midnight—
darkness hurried me—eyes destroy my tale—
the phoney telephone men, the cops—

my people bore me; bloody business!
Foul carcass rats have quit it,
bouncing and grinding along
through the brown dust, loving wrong.

Preserve me! Smile, stomach,
beating your reason upon a star,
a confetti of skulls and desert;
cease questions; dullness, and choose
an attack of paranoia.

Fly, swim, dive into the fire,
strong quality to every article—the drive-ins,
mobile home parks, septic tank developments,
raw concrete service station toilets, plaid car coats . . .

I deck, in amazement, and burn and flame
distinctly, then tremble, my mad son,
with hair like reeds, the devils close by—
waitresses looking like milky cellophane,
their garments cooling in this sad nook, where once
midnight hid; all asleep; and the trumpets
always dropping off the note.

Is there more moody liberty?

                    No more!

Remember I told lies, malignant age
hearing commands, refusing rage.
Then breasts undo art entrails.
Say what—

                  what shall I do?

Eyeball diligence! They will pay dearly
for the bullshit ambience. Shake fire, profit business—
poisonous devil, wicked cramps, night work, eat berries
that burn by day and night, secret poisonous orchid;
and then sipping beer and smoking many joints,
filth violate gabble like brutish words that learn
this rock, a prison, the red language!

Roar, tremble, pray,

                obey.

His art invisible, following yellow sands,
have kissed, bear dogs strutting,
my music gone. No, again lies;
his strange sound above me. The eye
looks about! It carries the grief, that's divine;
for I saw the daughter wrong a man, a virgin,
so great, a kind of brooding beauty,
and a spy—she wants to do this thing, but she does it
without belief. I am a man. He's a traitor. Follow.

No; I will resist such power.

                He's fearful.

Hush! No more shapes, moving the dark angels,
the subtropical twilights and soft westerlies
off the Pacific—nerves again, so much fire
concealed by the dark. My weakness,
threats in prison. A lot of people
had been worried that he was dead.
Every voice seems a scream.

                              Come on.

       §

Hang up a yellow shirt—you cause joy;
our escape is common; every day, some wife
masters our theme of preservation,
millions speak like us.

The visitor, he will strike the entertainer.
A dollar comes to him, you have taken his tongue,
the old laughter, though
that tawny eye of green misses
the truth totally, it was crazy, a kind of power.

She was the miraculous impossible matter.
We were as fresh as your daughter,
who is my sort. Your daughter's ears
against the stomach—her strange fish.

Thank yourself, bless your daughter, lose
an African—where is your eye?
Cause the grief to bow. Fear for ever,
prickly dread wherever the wind blows.
We bring men to your own loss.

You lack some time to speak, you rub the plaster.
Very well. And when you are very foul,
being drunk, no traffic, poverty of contract,
bound metal, or oil;
no men and women, no sweat.

Knife, gun, engine: prosper in the dry air,
feed my people. No subjects govern the age.
It is possible to live and die
without ever meeting a Catholic or a Jew.
Do you talk to these gentlemen?
They always laugh at nothing.
No one remembers the past—then go. I am heavy.
He talked about metaphysical paranoia—Shut up!

What a strange climate; glossy greenery
of nightmare, then my spirits fell by thunder.
What might I see in my head?
A place for snakes to breed. Do you hear me?

I do; and it is language,
and sleep.
            What is it?
                        This is strange, eyes open;
yet more serious than standing water.
Ebbing men near the bottom,
by their own birth, yield.

Although this memory is persuaded he's a spirit,
as he sleeps, I have another way: a hope, a wink,
he's gone.

Then tell me, who's beyond the sun?
Cry out—wake—he that sleeps
can amply make a deep chat.
O, you bore! What advancement!
Do you understand?
                    I do.
While you wink, the cat laps milk; we say the hour.

Dear precedent; I'll come free from love.
They talk, invisible; music and danger send me forth
to keep them snoring—keep care, beware
confidence of strange pygmy angel tribes.

The moon was dark and the wind was blowing.
We heard a hollow burst like bulls. It struck
a monster's ear, to make a humming, a strange one,
which cried; as I saw their weapons
there was a noise—that's our guard,
sobbing and incoherent. Quit our weapons,
for my poor beasts shall know what I have done.

From *Ultra* 2001

Lavender Ink

Look, there she is: Miss Bliss, dozing
in the shade of a Campari umbrella. Beside her
a book—something brilliant: Callimachus,
let's say, printed in an elegant Venetian type—
half-read, with the most alarming
        metaphors to come,

and a glass of gin, a cool dew
blooming on the crystal, the air
        kissing her skin
and the neighbour's hi-fi playing
'I Can't Get Started' in a distant
        corner of the afternoon.
The yachts on the water.
        The tinkle of ice.

I'm thinking of you reading this,
reinventing Sydney
a thousand years from now, and not
getting it quite right: missing the
delicate hangover, the distant murmur
of the city, the scent of this ink
        drying on the page.

Black Leather

They had returned to get the acoustic atmosphere
for the movie about the French criminals, recording
the soul of the place. When the narrative dissolved she felt
abandoned: first, as though her friends had walked out on her,
then in the other sense, loose, morally bankrupt.

It was an 'optimistic' picture, but dark.
The main writer fought with the story doctor,
refusing to answer his pained questions. They were
intellectuals, she shouted, don't you understand?
Working all night she developed strategies,

and gathered a close group of friends around her
to fend off the advances of the others, those
godless and tireless plotters. And the pages
whirling in the metallic light above the sand, the
waves and the pages folding and turning.

I could see her problem: the cranial arteries bulging,
bad culture gushing across the blood-brain barrier,
from the pages of soiled old books and splashy
magazines, a dozen new theories every month
boiling to the top of the heap of reprints.

Her students thought they had found a new leader,
the art pumping, and an innocent job, raking in money
and promotion. But the infection was linguistic,
and the form malevolent. She panted in the staff room
like a fly trapped in a Contents Page, struggling

with some half-dozen new hypotheses,
thinking she was checking them out, but
they were doing the checking, sorting out
the designer theories, the gangs of black-clad youths
hunting down the latest clever chat.

Her work was growing stunted and corrupt
but fluent for all that, and people bought it.
The skyrocket of fashion, it's not evil, she said,
it can be useful, even for the working class,
look, they bask in the light from its burning tail.

That's how culture floats on the lake
of civilisation, its image wavering in the hazy air.
She thought of her certain extinction—no—
you'll always win if you can predict how
the dog will jump, her script doctor said.

Memo: When I began decoding the images
unravelling from the screen I thought I was
reading your heart print, but I'd been fooled.
Woman does not have a Soul for a reason,
you argued, it's not the product of evolution,

that fashion for splitting up the dead, they so many,
into burnt or heavenly pensioners, that is vicious,
can't you see that? The projector flickering,
the pages signed with her name curling
in the heat, blackening and bursting into flame.

Gallery

The teachers would hammer us into artists,
recalcitrant base metal beaten into gold,
if they could. To me, joy-rides were art,
and ploughing was a type of inscription—
I hear behind the droning motor someone's

childhood weathered away and wasted, the boy
in the threadbare snotty jacket hating us
for noticing him thus, and his blame becomes
his chief addiction, a flush of resentment,
about how others pushed and bullied.

Who's pushing? The theory that pretends to be
no theory at all, it was busy blocking that other
theory, disordered, quarrelling, quickly finished with,
his royal madness noted spotting plots behind the bushes,
sobbing with rage, a devotee of the sulky air.

I lived in grace, and fell into poisoned maturity—
seaside cabins packed with wicked kids drinking—
a world of bush farms turned into a landscape.
To read it, you just moved forward into it.
They call those mountains a 'horizon', which is only

a boundary, not a thing. Parents were templates,
but I could not plot the father. A spanner
clinked on steel and danced in the ringing shed.
The tractor did its work like any rusty mechanism
and his office was the open air, a church of absence.

He wore old blue things. Does history
have to be past tense? The diary says I'm
older than he ever got to be, can it be true?
In a fragment of dream chatter I
catch my voice from another room and hear

my father's laugh. Is he here? He's been dead—
'I had the shivers—lock the back door.' Broken
now—pack away Hope, his poem of the future.
I photographed myself, I drank the rain
in deep gulps in flooded February.

Driving to a party, young people, that cheap kiss
traded for a magazine with torn covers.
High on killing ethylene, I realised
wrong could be right. They'd punish the boys
to save them. I would not join.

You had to take a girl to the dance, or
you were a creep, the guys opined anxiously.
And her? She wanted to be a debutante,
though she knew the routine was a farce.
Kids growing at their own pace, by the river.

The old men forbade the barbecue, and now
a thunderstorm begins with pattering drops,
laughter, girls' dresses bunched under the shelter,
the grey sky stretching so far, impossibly distant,
where I glimpse myself longing to go home.

Halogen

A cold wind came into the room, it frightened
everyone. It was not only that the temperature
dropped, that chill air blew against my skin, but
now the outside was invading the cute domestic space,
something horrible was blundering in,

a taste of death, a slavering alien, those were the
fucking metaphors that Brain-Damage here
was babbling before she fell onto her martini glass
and cut her abdomen on the broken shards,
the lemon stinging in the wound.

Yes, this is the new lingo, brazen, disfigured,
named after those serrations on the kitchen knives
whose cutting edge is etched by a blade of light, that
apparatus glittering on the altar of the bourgeoisie,
dazzled with adjectives and halogen lights.

You didn't make up with him—there, are you
going to say the whole disaster was my fault, you,
tête-à-fucking-tête with the guard dog on the patio?
Straighten up! I'm not interested in the cave
where your teddy bears are projected on a wall,

the velvet manacles and the various bottles.
Now the open road—grainy black and white—
collapsed, separated by photos, the family sobbed,
shark eat shit and they should never have to read about it
and they had to read about it because your bad deeds

follow you home, the ashamed pattern
slipping down the stairs and colliding with reality.
I'd been within voice range of that wreckage,
cramped by journalism, the politics of friends
reviewing each other in the weekend papers.

It's simply a kindness, isn't it, but looked at
from over the fence, a slick fall from honour.
Friends laughed it off, others were aghast, the critics
said it was greed, and how come I couldn't tell
the difference? Then in the garden, two people

behind the screen, the peaks reflecting late sunlight,
poison into the very mouth, then the necessary nausea
as mustard is pumped in to bring other stuff out,
is there an economy in that?
or a loss of faith? They

were gaping at the wounds in my stomach.
For weaklings, it was too much.
They had slept under the desert moon,
the kiss of the mirror, but under that problem
were others, made visible when the lamps arrived,

head over heels in love, then a sharp pain, and I
made excuses to the medium's creep forward in time.
Then she'd be interested in that reality solicit,
the movies cranking out their smoky humour.
Then everything dissolves, down the river.

Locket

Her laugh had shocked her university friends.
She would have to find a faith in a bottle,
the dark never really dark, but her life story
more like a riddle at the bottom of the glass
calling the loonies in across the lawns.

Crazy smile—I'm a bit of surgery,
this is not my real career, he said; I'm a jockey—
tracing the tram track it followed—my life,
not myself. And worse, his brain was a dick,
that's how he described it. Cut to the economy

of the street, they were just bad, those
cruising boys, the bay now a body locker,
on the nearby slopes a homestead or two,
no traffic on the grass, only on bitumen because
appropriate—driving around in her dad's car and her

usual daze like a robot on Sunday, the slow traffic
photographing how it is reflected as a carnival
by the strips of dusty glass, how the murmur
has a querulous inflection, the tone the Tang poets
struggled to get down on paper, once they'd invented it—

ages ago. She had taken her name from a ribbon,
a name tag that offered a motto—*loser*.
Then when she broke open the fortune cookie,
the message gave the proof of Fermat's last theorem,
wasted here among the groggy customers.

They were busy calling blue jokes out
to one another in the toilets, yelling through
green glass, and tawny lemon, and the scent
of that cheap hospital grade disinfectant
and she answered: *I'm listening to that,*

you jerks! From a neighbouring cubicle
then—a smaller moment than many—
I knew that she'd sob, that her good times
had ended, that she seemed the strangest creature
to herself. It was so lonely there, in the suburbs

fringing the university, the passing crowd
full of brainy Australian intellectuals who,
once they'd been indoctrinated thoroughly,
had all turned into their own doubles—like that.
She stumbled on her high heels, maybe she would have

developed into a genius, who knows, and her friends
were shocked when the Chinese waiter brought her home,
back early from the old testament, and babbling scribble,
stretched out from each week's work, remember disentangle
her mad laugh at the dark, then looking through the car

for her makeup. Her laugh echoed under the trees,
the lamplit street sleeping, now a dog spoke,
the moon sinking behind the distant ridge,
her university friends abandoned long ago,
along with her childhood—marriage—the locked locket.

Miss Proust

To her the kissing group of husbands and wives
was like a gang of schoolgirls in the laundry,
all fuss and bother, with no proper theory of how
sexuality is conditioned by the economic
strictures of society, and not by the games shows

and the sporting programs or by the lies
that stain the pages of cheap paper, for example,
when her friends told her she was a rotten writer—
fuck it!—plumping up the pillow of her emotions—
so she could feel in love—click on, click off—

and revel in a moody air in the kitchen, scribbling
diary entries as though they were great roiling thoughts
or worse, riveting literature, meant to be read out
during the long night of the adult education course
training tapping dogs to do the new job, it's obviously

made for love, this mechanical device with its ribbon
spooling out reams of confectionery and duplicity
that young women desperately want to believe
could happen to them, like doctors who are stern and rich—
no, *will* happen to them—and the pretty nurses

who are young and whimpering, but somehow dazzling,
the same story, only glowing with a more literary quality—
now it happens, only the ending is wrong,
and the hero, called Bruce or Duane, is a loser—
there are no doctors here, they live elsewhere

with their wives, their investments, and their matched
pairs of children. We went over the story—
in the magazine with the doll on the cover—
her writing was okay, it pulled in the money, but
the 3-D Speed Queen routine she put on

mainly for the benefit of the mirror, that was relatively
thrilling, and her hair, so expensive, like snakes—dark
and full of movement. I've spent a lot
on these magazines, the shameful ones, and
often longed to be a maker of such spectacles,

my hand writing out a kind of existentialism
of the glands—clashing or cooperating—keen
to be liked, anxious to find a friend,
weary of the endless social gambits, sad to admit
the need for wariness and protective latex devices.

I was like a wave in a tiny dry-point etching,
apparently calm on the surface, distressed underneath.
I know it is no excuse, but that angry remark
that was changed into something cool and polished,
like an aphorism, isn't that a betrayal of the emotion

that produced it? Isn't it cultural greed reified,
and turned into a regular income? Answer me,
you little shit! There you are, sobbing,
hiding under a pile of theories in the corner,
dabbing at your makeup and hoping not to be noticed.

My Story

Back in *la belle époque* the hired hand would spend
all his savings on a wireless, and turn a cold shoulder
to the investment bloopers of the rural poor.
You learn enough to get along, the rest
is embroidery bracketing mushy urban wishes.

Stared at by the sun some freckled tomboy
wants to buy a drink, but she drops her change—
a coin rolls into the gutter and down the drain,
unimagined voyages to distant Floridas strapped
to the wheel of the will, where the water boils

in the teeth of the hurricane—never to happen,
dark and cold while the centuries roll overhead.
Now some rustic is rubbing my face
with his nicotine-stained fingers. Token?
They won't remember what the cycle meant.

Winter nights . . . the village draws the snow rug
around its knees, the lamps whisper nostalgic
baloney from one side of the street to the other,
the old schoolteacher peers at his book—
the book which talks of glory, and later

he'll be reduced to getting drunk on beer and
watching football through a tube—
Think of an accordion bought and sold—boy,
it must have seen some parties! Or imagine good times,
bad times, around the pianola. A rat doesn't need

a degree in entomology, he just carries the plague,
it's his talent and his gift. This is just one coin,
but it speaks for its millions of brothers, gazing
down on the planet through the polished
lens of commerce: tides, movements,

the harbour mouth silting up. It must be
phenomenal to be a farmer, every nerve in your body
in touch with the seasonal interest rate fluctuations,
doing your bit to clog the rivers and pollute the earth,
and, given a flexible borrowing rate, able

to rent a light plane to spread insecticides
almost on a whim—ploughman as artist. Now
the bond ratio climbs, now a family
plunges into debt and alcohol,
now the Red Man is pressed from this

part of the West, miles of waving sorghum
cover what was once a prairie, now in Kalamazoo
a bookkeeper plots to bring down a bank.
The earth revolves, hiding its secrets. I may sleep
for a million years, and when I turn up at last

my value will be infinite, or nothing. What drugs
will replace me? My story, a sixpence
shaped like the moon, always standing in
for someone else, the soft suffering flesh
put behind me, part of a stupendous machine.

Off Radar

I tried selling—a dog would sell better.
Then I dived into escape, relaxation—
westerns, flirting at the local dance, cheap
fiction, I said I was an expression of the times,
nothing more—bring a jug of water—

and the hicks spinning on the sawdust floor
believed me, drinking in the music, the glitter and
the harsh saxophone ambience which belongs
to our century, the minor chords Bach didn't know—
because artists feel more deeply they have a special

right to authentic orgasm—enough teaching,
I know the law as nails understand
the hammer—my focus set at the horizon,
racking in the light, inch by inch by inch
then the sun came up, the sky a deep blue—

what happened out there, it was not so much
a hairstyle as a wig, and this kind of thing
happened to Australian art every year,
talent moulting, sheep sheltered from the sun,
fading like the shadow of a phobia, less nexus,

more periphery—one daydream concerned
the pitch-black truck manoeuvre, the acid bath.
Again and again how sheer the brand-names
and cliché kisses, boycott knocked rocking—
you can't wrench free of the devised world—

there's my wife, sad old neighbourhood angel,
she never got jealous, never ran down the other,
the innocent one—God help me—blizzards
that he believed made her happy, an arm
around her, is that sad moment over?—hey

sweetheart, did your husband hear the boy paint?
I drew on pliable acetate, now it's
a subtle cheater, where my ambition
was to have a stimulant stab at his work,
my shirt pocket full of pencils, brain

full of plans for escape from the Lawn Club,
the wives gathering around to graze and feast
on my exoticism, but that was accidental, not
fundamental, back home I was a nobody,
when I need to I can swear to that, and

when it suits me I can be that other person.
I return to the inner sky and the screen flickers,
then clears—they say art tore their spirits to bits—
their howls came after the furiously sobbing girls
woke up to find themselves in their sixties—

mayhap in my childish breast the clock,
an artifice that suffocates—wallpaper, perfume, I'd
cancel the jasmine-scent of radar writing and that's
nothing compared to what we find at the end:
a ring from the little bell on the front of a bike.

On the Road

We met at the bar concealed behind a false front
in the alley behind a curtain dyed purple and green
down the stairs to the shuttered room baking
in the Summer of Love, a country girl, dark glasses,
thirty feet of cedar bar stacked with drinks

but we already had those drinks, and it seems
in the pool of liquid on the bar surface,
after I finished pawing at her soft willing body,
I could see the outline of a face. Too close.
She joined a big city firm, designing perfume,

can you believe, and she used to say 'You have
a soul, in the Big Town, because people let you live.'
Why are these problems linguistic?
That's all we have, to frame the chaos with,
the big grid we drank with our mothers' milk

with the cornflakes and the funerals. This went on
in front of the runaway truck of culture
loaded with 'fashion', that abstract policeman.
It's the beach, dozing on the edge of my mind,
a life hung loose by the water, a giggle of a man

mumbling about the knife-edge of darwinism
hacking at our schools, and what was in the sand,
kids punching each other in the surf—
now from the back of the bar the lost cry
of someone losing out to the sixties, coded

into the static you can hear hissing in the car radio—
God and the Sheriff sharing a good cigar,
entente cordiale, agreeing they love a dash of
green, humanised water with their bourbon.
One chemical strips the other of information,

mingling in the tank of brew. It was lonely,
in the banking business, like a convalescent pushing
a truck uphill, inch by inch, and dog eat dog
in the bull pit, wondering who had the trend brackets
with the right linguistic spin to win.

Then that maelstrom of bad writing
calling students to their doom. 'I didn't
disillusion my poor charges,' the old guy sobbed.
Why do I remember this? He was too much
like me, and I saw my father in the mirror,

growing sad, he had a tale to tell me urgently,
but I couldn't hear, or stay to listen.
I moved out of bohemia, Kerouac went mad there,
that's a lesson, then he died at his mother's,
that's another lesson, to do with philosophy,

Catholic childhoods, bad drink, Oedipus.
I dreamed to cope, and I'd seen what happened,
in the future, like a train becoming larger.
'Here in the present we're just waiting for history
to run us down. Teachers cannot help us.'

Package Tour

There's a gap electricity leaks across
between the eyeball and the page, between
the demonstrator showing off the dicing knife
and the tired woman going home on the train.
For five million people Paris is a place to work,

not a fucking vacation. So the young flirt
went to Europe, meaning to spend her money.
Cigarette packets, rain showers, Existentialism
blowing through the groups of confused tourists—
whistling some tune, these prisoners of air,

a sad little melody that spelled out how
lost they were, under the European weather.
She walked in the rain, the acid drench
that was pouring on the new wet paint,
wading through sheets of green gauze.

Her anxiety was quickly dispatched, and the messages
soon sparked down the wire to clang the bell
back home. The hot air was shuddering, they said
it was necessary—voice flattened by the phone—
to make an example of the rapist feller;

and the girl reporter read about it on the Teletype
and came down here looking for trouble.
We gave her trouble, more than she planned on.
Click. I guess it was some family habit.
She was working class, all right.

You could tell, under the cunning accent
she put on, something hollow, stained, fake.
Everything in the kitchen could be overheard.
To paint—that's all she wanted to do,
even if was just grasping lies.

You could take it that this was only a moral lesson,
or you could imagine more. That's up to you.
She pushed the doors open, looking in
at the confused diners, and only a moment ago
she'd been fascinated by history's obsession with itself,

how we stayed up and talked till dawn
when we were just dumb kids, like philosophers.
She drank ouzo and retsina until even the Greeks
wouldn't have any more of her, drank
till dawn, threw up, then drank some more.

It had been raining in the square,
the cobbles were slick, and coming home
from another binge, she slipped, twisted her
ankle and knocked out a tooth on the kerb.
So the biographer says.

She wore a raincoat everywhere, a matter of
style, to work, to the toilet, God knows, and
when she let it slip to the floor the buckle clacked
on the tiles. She saw her future rise up, a sheet
of lightning. Paris or Peoria, it's all the same.

Per Ardua ad Astra

I was thinking about what happened when you were
a kid, the theft of capital, how the bottle
came uncorked, and how the precious essence
of capitalism simply turned into vapour
and disappeared, destroying whole nations.

It was bookkeeping made it happen,
we should blame the strings of numbers holding
hands, and the passion to build a toy that works.
Capital, it just grows out of the world's matter—
a nugget, a heap of rice, a busload of workers.

I always had my staff learn only the essentials.
More than that, and they develop longings.
Perhaps a Buddhist could offer a better response
to the way the economy is like a ravening animal,
wounding and maiming the poor.

But then, the stragglers have to get picked off,
is that what you said? So let's armour ourselves,
let's get a degree in little things, like courtesy
and social stratagems, how to knot a rhyme,
and dazzle the old ladies with our manners.

The first year I knew her she gave me
the entire history of her mind from go to whoa,
how she faced up to the great cliffs
of European culture, that had destroyed
more than one civilisation, and might do again.

She was confused by truth when it is stacked up into
blocks of history, though not by the lies that
make up politics. I'd been fascinated with mahogany jazz,
you know the stuff, disturbing, dark, but mellow—
but we only heard a mournful song play, and

as the harmonies tangled deliciously and then
unravelled they seemed to say no, to forbid
a country girl to have such thrilling insights.
Or literature, the alphabet pretending to some
great passion, one more bourgeois jerk

raking in the dollars while he tapped at the keys,
constructing a profiterole cloud-castle of emotion—
as vital as a college diploma, this talent for cheating—
though what chance that had of persuading anybody—
no, I'm not jealous—give it a rest—the nerves—

'Neal was enormously attractive to people
who sat on their ass most of the day in a dim room,
biting their nails, and typing out shit.' That's
what he said. He was a big handsome feller,
thick as a brick, whacked on speed most times,

and faintly talented. I couldn't get him hunting, the old
President said—what he was afraid of was a mystery to me,
shaking while the sound travelled low over the ground,
reading The Declaration of Independence through
the telescopic sight on the barrel of a gun.

South Farm

You get yourself a beer from the fridge, pour a glass,
and stand, watching the froth settle, remembering—
or you're leafing through a magazine at the dentist's,
and you see a colour photo of a fox in a forest—
I was after this fox, he said, looked everywhere.

Clever bastards, they know more than you do.
I must have walked four miles through the bush.
I took a rest on this big hollow log. Lovely morning,
dew on the grass, everything quiet. I rolled a smoke,
very peaceful. Heard a noise, looked around,

and the bloody fox shot out of the log
and off into the bracken. I just laughed.
Remember? Dad's laugh had a special resonance,
his voice, relaxed, the rhythm of breath—I hear it
sometimes, now that he's gone, long gone

from the land of the living, smoke up the chimney,
I hear it sometimes at a party, from the next room,
and I go in to look, anxious, excited—no,
there's no one there, except myself in the mirror.
The drink—it's just something to get you started,

breaking the ice of the held-in talk. He said
a rabbit would stretch the meagre rations
during the war—which war?—baked in milk, very
palatable. And the old radio on the kitchen table
was thronged with the noise of the city celebrating,

far away behind the eucalyptus-crowded hills,
and yet close enough to touch. The traffic drone
came from behind the scenery, the urban horizon,
fixed about so high, and there were closer sounds—
talk, murmurs, the noise of people shopping.

Are you just passing by? I whispered—for they
had an odd look: just visiting the planet—aren't we all?
And that struggle, growing up, dying,
what does it matter now? His son
had read the story he particularly liked—

the whish of passing tyres on the street outside
seemed to spell out a message—that he was doomed
to linger in this dim room, lonely, bored,
trying to understand the television that seemed to be
speaking another language to the furniture

until he could be rescued by his family—only
one problem—he didn't have any family.
I am my father's son. In the empty kitchen
the crockery was cold, the dishwasher had stopped
long ago, the detective reasoned—he'd retired

from his position examining the books
for this so-called library, what a laugh, and now
he was raking over the detritus of a life spent
trying to farm stubborn soil. Take me
back to my real parents. I am that detective.

Under the Trees

The boy had been killed, an accident, and how
his parents lived on is hard to understand.
The teacher wiped her misted glasses primly,
and we wheeled our bikes down that long empty road.
My dad, he cranked the handle, holding his thumb

in a special grip he taught me, useless gift,
and the truck started in a cloud of blue smoke.
The candor—that thing I am aiming at—
pungent smoke, memory trace, the jacket—
the no man's land between what I meant to say

and my doleful history—that gap, slot, error—
a body down there in the gully, or floating
in the dam, the boy stumbled on the step
between master and mister, a dreadful threshold.
Stunned, down there among the bracken, resting

just on twilight, then the teacher's broken voice
climbing up through the aether—this ascent
is like a plane, equivalent of hope rising
the way the sunrise gets plants awake—
now just a whistle rising through the static.

The old bell made us wait, life piling up
on the steps outside. How does it matter now?
'My brother,' he said, 'volunteered for service
in the fire brigade, but he was one of them,
the wicked ones, lighting fires and putting them out.'

When they caught him—one story, just one,
from all those countless texts that shape a pearl
layer by paper-thin layer, trochus embroidery,
watered silk of his moods, this is literature?
Under the floor a manuscript rolled up

and tied with string and sealed with wax,
just talk from the city, café babble, passions
nudging at the future like a fish in a bottle
I remember, condemned by the invisible wall,
why didn't I apprehend the future? Tomorrow and

tomorrow staggering into life, and plans
aborted each evening, then an accident to prove
you shouldn't have wanted anything.
You drive past the tree split by lightning
holding up its arms, a piece of burnt wood

in the figure of a ghost watching the forest
as the rain colours the world dark grey and glossy,
something is waiting under the branches, an alien spirit,
the ghastly revenant invaders feel, their own reflection
projected on the ruin they have made.

But looking back, the photograph album, sepia
waterfalls, a wasteland of dead white trees,
the dusty ferns and the cane furniture—outside
in the sun, two magpies quarrelling, saying
'today is all that exists, and be grateful for it.'

From *Borrowed Voices* 2002

After Laforgue

I light a cigarette under the moon
and fling myself onto the grass, inhaling, inhaling:
trees without flowers, flowers without nectar,
nectar without alcohol: I wish you were here
beside me, I'd talk until you were dizzy.

What was wrong with me, in my previous life?
Ardent, steely, mercurial—angry again.
I was in a fit of love, but I couldn't admit it,
and as for you: bellicose, unreachable,
as self-contained as a wardrobe with its vanity mirror
on the shut side of the door . . . you
with your expensive little knapsack
and your plans for your singular future . . .
up there the stars are as plentiful as all the possible
games of chess, according to the scholarly apparatus,
according to the guard with his cap, lamp and whistle.

Married to my obligations I swim in the harbour,
and if I'm too fussy for happiness to visit
let me bathe in my luck—good or bad—
my wretched luck, if that's all that's on offer.
One day, far into the future, I'll come to my senses:
cruising down the main street of a small town
where the moon, jealous of the abundant lighting,
draws the selvage of a cloud across her brow.

Now I speak in letters of Greek Fire
the better to spark your indifference, to
draw down your scorn—I mean admiration,
O princess of fisticuffs: intricate patterns of vowels,
spells that sparkle and promise to outlast metal—
speak to you, in your boots, in your jacket, in the
steel car you drive through the shell of your future.

Brussels

(a version of Rimbaud's 'Brussels')

The eagle who kills with lightning
idles in a palace smothered by flowers.
Of course he is never seen. The sky above is
pale green and Saharan blue, shreds and patches of it
peeping between the dark leaves . . .

it must be the Côte d'Azur, it must be fast cars,
idle young men inflamed by gasoline!
And when the exhaust note has faded, why,
calm returns, the last century returns, my
abandoned world returns, the world I have lost,

the life I threw away, the Juliet I neglected—
can any of that be recovered? Blue devils
topple from gliders into a pattern: parachutes,
idols, descending . . . history is this delicious day
over and done—old orchards: forgotten fruit.

Now the waterfront, patrolled by helicopters,
where monkeys dance, guitars pluck at the air,
children in red makeup clutch at your sleeve,
and, looking down from a secluded window
a beautiful woman dazed by magazines . . .

renting an exclusive suite done out
like a library, books bound in buckram, so she can
doze on a divan, nothing more useful: nothing
more ravishing than her vulnerable sleep—let us
creep and whisper! Below, a cul-de-sac choked with

expensive shops towards whose glow and glitter
her soul inclines, whose chandeliers illuminate
her heaven, whose throngs act out a million dramas
curt, cruel, and concentrated, just for her: I dwell on it—
be jealous!—and adore it in silence.

Address to the Reader

(after Veronica Forrest-Thomson)

In the art of sinking into a landscape
or falling through the sky, a light touch
moves you to sympathy, or a deeper knowledge
of a heroine's little faults.
Now the Riddle of the Sands
argues with its history,
fiddles with a likely clue and abandons it.
In the stone passageway, a pointer:
chalk marks indicate a track, a working man
dawdles and leans on a shovel
reading a notice about submerged structures
that may yet transform this deliquescent scene
into an emotional instruction manual—that is,
the meaning layer is read into it or varnished
onto it, a melancholy murmur
heard even in France in winter: a longing
for interpretation. Follow those emblematic persons
through their countryside, turning into your townscape
built of crooked curves and negative camber;
for to be true to your dreams you must—
here blotted words—recover
a young person's knack known as
departure through the mirror of sleep.

After Rilke

(a version of Rilke's 'First Duino Elegy')

I hate this place. If I were to throw a fit, who
among the seven thousand starlets in Hollywood
would give a flying fuck? Or suppose some tired
studio executive, taken by my boyish beauty—no,
I'd suffocate. Charm is only makeup-deep,
I reckon, and staring in the mirror too long
can give you the horrors: that thing in the glass,
it doesn't care. Every nymphette burns
for some drug or other. I'm not drinking tonight,
do you mind? Messages banking up, unanswered.
On the screen a masked cowboy chases
a masked cowboy: the moonlit glade
is black and white. Even here among the big-wigs
the servants are unreliable, the pool
fills up with foliage and seagull droppings.
Who'll clean it up? Not the top brass, not
the Mexican gardener raking leaves in the drive,
who sees how uneasy we are reading the headlines
and the newsreels' various interpretations
of the shit going on in Europe.

The trees just grow—that cypress,
a black finger scraping the blue, or the dry palmettos
decorating Sunset's long slope to the Pacific, fronds
rattling in the breeze—they say rats nest in them,
their pink babies safe from harm—grow like a habit
that takes root in a tangle of frailties and becomes
as regular as rum in the morning coffee. And the stars
glimmering through the smog, and the night wind,
see how it ruffles the hair of a snoring beggar.
Now, standing on the pier at Santa Monica,
looking out over all that black water, I'm appalled

by the way errant birds are caught in the lights
and seem no more than fluttering scraps of paper.
Up the slope from the beach in a lamplit hacienda
in the Spanish Mission style, a violin
is crying its guts out: some good Jewish kid
pleasing his mama; Carnegie Hall his given task.
I need a severe love like that, those demands
that tell me someone wants to suck my blood;
me with my big head, and my dealers always
coming and going through the French windows,
wrecking the flower-bed. I'm not well—
and when I want a doctor I want a good one,
some overgrown whiz-kid who can
knock up an aorta from a length of garden hose,
and immortalize the alchemy of surgery
on the cover of *Time* magazine. Let me praise
the tired GP with his pad of blank prescriptions:
hero to the working poor, sucker to junkies—
what am I talking about?
                              We were cowboys,
hacienda, moonlight—the letter zee
as the alphabet's last occasion for self-assertion—
but Zorro in his guise of landed gentry
sits up till dawn alone in the library
comparing his first editions of Cervantes,
one mis-bound and paginated incorrectly,
the other almost perfect—exhausted yet fulfilled.
I could be like him, whining in the harness-shed,
snapping at the groom in English—time to get out,
an arrow loosed high over suburbia . . . I'll
die, stuck here . . .

                    Voices and echoes
from the mantel radio, slow jazz at midnight—
mental radio—I remember the recording engineer
bent over his control panel, focused,
the swooning harmonies lifting him from the ground—
no, his bloodshot eyes are locked on the meters,
watching the headroom—and the saxophone
calling from the past: the voice of a young god.

I know those notes, that particular melodic twist:
he died young and he will be young forever,
his picture on the record covers talking to me,
the black disk revolving—what does he
want from me? What can I say
to undo ruin, what could I have said
to mend that broken story?

There he is, a pattern in the stars, perhaps:
a slight alteration in those haughty diagrams.
Strange, to inhabit the sky at last, discarding
his spare change and his car keys,
his body left behind like a broken toy.

And me, and me—the pier locked for the night,
stars wheeling above, street lights below,
light calling to light, distant harmonies
across the long reaches of grief, moonlight
in monochrome calling me to sleep.

Invitation to America

(a version of Baudelaire's 'Invitation to the Voyage')

It's a day for daydreaming: rain
choking the gutters, wind whistling at the window.
Put down that coffee for a minute
and think about it—a ménage à deux
at the other end of the planet, floating on a culture
with a blank mind, or rather, surfing
on the waves of fashion, asleep on the wing,
splashed by each passing trend.

The way the sun lifts up from the backdrop
so enthusiastically and lights up the windblown
clouds from behind, it's a knockout,
a patchwork canopy of blue and yellow.

The storekeepers, the cops, the culture vultures
remind me of you—deliquescent con-artist,
blinking and lying through the convenient tears.
Like a paint job on a new convertible
the talk is brilliant and skin-deep.
No history—who needs it? The furniture
seems to know what you're planning, day by day,
the air conditioning blesses you with perfume,
the mirrors are discreet in what they remember
and what they choose to forget.

The vernacular of the shopping channel
and the sale catalog is on everybody's lips—
nothing but beauty and elegance, and the houseboats
and the matching housecoats are just right!
Along the canals, the clink of ice-blocks knocking
in a jug, the traffic lights are only ever green or amber,
and the big orange moon rises on cue,
haunt of astronauts. Think about it:

a voyage that takes you to yourself;
a movie that reminds you of its own locale.

On La Cienega

(a version of Schiller's 'A Maiden from Afar')

By the filling station on La Cienega a burger joint
somehow survives. This Sunday morning
a pink Thunderbird sags at the kerb,
and an old Studebaker, paint flaking.

Suzy got a job waitressing there, she doesn't quite
remember how or when. She turns up for work
just as the first bus trundles by, shifting gears
at the corner, the double diesel's throaty roar
making the plate glass tremble and glitter.

She didn't come from around there—nobody did.
'I left the Midwest—don't ask me when,'
she said once. This morning she gets the key
and goes to the john. The empty sky
has that pale hazy look that means a hot day.

I like it when she stops to talk awhile.
She brings a second cup of coffee, and
'You should try the espresso,' she says. 'God,
I could do with a drink.' But with the boss watching
she makes sure to smile at the customers:

old Ed with yesterday's paper, the bag lady
from down at the Marina, who used to be
a Hospitality Executive, if you can believe that,
even that wasted couple in the corner
rubbing their arms and not noticing anything:

not the spilled milk, not the cigarette burning down
between the girl's fingers, not even the view
through the speckled window: the hills
covered with dry scrub, and in the parking lot
a cop checking out their rusting car
and talking on the radio. I can't stand

losers like that. 'They just got married,' Suzy whispers,
wiping the counter and looking over her shoulder at them.
Then she takes the little vase of flowers from
next to the cash register and puts it on their table—

and of course they don't notice, the girl biting her nails,
the guy staring into his plate—some daisies
that she'd picked from a neighbor's yard
and a sprig of freesias the color of cream and butter
whose dreamy scent competes with coffee and gasoline.

Festival

(a version of Max Jacob's 'Festival')

As the mirror ball turns and sparkles, a rainbow
of opalescent light speaks code along the spine
of the calcified skeleton in the display case, colors
that light up the haze floating above the crowd of drunks.

On the fringe, a gang of five angry women
whose eyes flash at the thought of a missed meal,
who spot a new guest, sizing him up—
game, for a duel, fit to be hated or adored

and pampered for a while, dissembled with, then
skewered on a phrase—or is he perhaps
the fiery devil they were each waiting for
stretched out on the divans, meat on the grill?

In another room palm readers with degrees
in Boolean logic solve the Travelling Salesman Problem
or the 'maximal clique problem' over a drink, then
turn to the plentiful supply of delegates

who have brought briefcases choked with fright:
a childhood spent sweating in a cupboard,
an adolescence that was a long fainting fit,
a marriage touched with torture, a garden of shames—

these victims wait shaking in the lobby where the waiters
circle with trays of pale green glasses, hoping to find
a new life in the lines of their hands, and rise above it all.
I asked the fortune teller why I seemed to be here,

and got no useful answer, except for his sudden
and surprising avowal of passion, which in my case—
according to the logical calculations—seemed
an investment without hope of a tangible return.

Night

(a version of Vicente Huidobro's 'Night')

A whirring contraption whispers across the snow
in an outlying suburb of my anxiety;
lamps everywhere, and at their feet pools of light
and icy brine in a slurry. The scent of frying meat.
A tangle of cassette tape hooked on a branch
catches bits of glittery moonshine—
so much for the entertainment industry.

You, in your fur coat and the other luxury
accoutrements harvested from pawn shops,
you seem to burn with a strange heat,
your bare shoulders are steaming slightly,
and your contemptuous look ignites my cigar—

voices in the fog, a man and a girl,
something about 'foreign affairs' —

luckily the harbour's full of fishing boats
to distract me from further gloomy insights.
A bird scouts the wreckage, a mast tilts
as a ferry passes, pointing to this constellation,
then that. Which star will answer my hot wishes,
which one will rain down ruin?

It's bad luck to whistle, so I whistle.
The ring my old flame gave me
for remembrance—what was her name?
Rosa?—catches a glint from a street light.
The artfully cut garnet gleams rose-purple—
that, and the firefly of my cigar:
two stars on my fingers for luck.

Harry's Bar

(after Callimachus)

By the time the stranger turned up at Harry's Bar
down by the waterfront, and slumped into a seat
under a fan, in the back room, he was badly winded—
but by what, exactly, he couldn't say.

He gave a little gasping sound when
the third shot of whiskey hit the target.
'Ah, that's better,' he was heard to remark brightly,
as a few pink petals fell from the stupid wreath

he was wearing, and scattered on the floor.
Visions of bliss, apparently—dreams
of happiness to rival shopping
filled his horizon. 'Winged,' he sighed,

to no one in particular, 'Love
ambushed me. Bugger it!'
Trying to pass it off as a flesh wound,
when in fact he was shot to pieces.

Writing down the scene, it seems to me
that there's a pattern there:
a blueprint I can decipher all too easily,

having come to understand the complaint
more or less like one of the walking wounded, like
one of the victims, as it were.

What the Cyclops Said

(after Callimachus)

[   ] poets have two remedies
against Love's engineer—Hunger,
that lives in their pockets, and
their (intoxicating?) Muse.

So, Cupid, petrol-scented boy,
[   ] (back to?) your chariots,
[   ] your business with axle-grease!
We have a double remedy against you!

Where the Boys Are

(after Callimachus)

Waking up, I'm half man, half headache
with half my soul dead or vanished,
or maybe gone to Florida, carried off
in a fever. Once, before the Age of Latex
and Heavy Metal, kisses were kisses,
not infections. Has my ninth life
gone again to amble, sunstruck,
where the boys are? But I begged them
not to give shelter to the runaway slave—
'Turn him out onto the street!'—*fat chance!*—
I'm searching here among the crowd of trash
in the back room behind the bar—won't you
help? He's here, somewhere, with the bad boys,
half a star looking for an answering flame,
hunting, restless, and ripe for death.

Notes from the Late Tang

for Jeremy Prynne

On the mountain of (heaped snow, boiled rice)
I met Tu Fu wearing a straw hat against the midday sun
distant bridge, restless parting, rain (in, on) the woods
[line missing]

willows among white clouds (shirt, chemise, ghost)
(to take the long view) parting
away moving, mobile telephone handset
[Bob: perhaps that's 'grief at parting']

my humble (borrowed, not inherited)
cottage (pig-sty) perspective
there is a misty view (of, from?) bridge
the storm took three layers of thatch, so

rain through the roof, porcine lucubrations
(something?) pig oil study
[Bob: 'pig oil' can't be right]
burning the midnight oil in my study

phantom liberty, ghost freedom view
great ancient poet wrote for radio
(would have written) had he known
(subjunctive) radio receiver, milkmaid attitude

silkscreen pastoral, pants metaphor
looking back, sorrow (shopping) lady
parting (hair) long voyage
light and green woods, little pig woman

[Bob: I think that's 'young swineherd girl']
she questions (annoys) the lonely traveller
unfortunate view (of, from)
pig liquid telephone handset

From *Studio Moon* 2003

Moonshine Sonata

I come to, knocking on the door of the cellar—
locked up for the summer—where you keep your 'heart'.
But isn't that the parcel you passed
to some likely guy, a neighbourhood fellow,
one spring day full of showers and confetti,
in between mowing the lawn in a check shirt
and making sensible plans for your retirement?
Why don't you ask for it back, wrapped
in plastic—we could take it with us on our
vacation from the feelings we wade through
each evening, in our separate rooms.
                    Then I really
wake up, and there I am: painting
the skylight amber to filter the glare
that shines on the Southern Hemisphere,
and when the record stops, it's your turn:
Love & Marriage, say, or *Frenesi*,
but not the Moonshine Sonata
                    in his black jacket
gusting across Broadway in a flurry of snow.

The Twilight Guest

First, she purchased
a little cottage by the lake—
fresh-water, not salt—
and sat waiting for poetry.
No one but the sunlight came wandering
down the lane. The atmosphere
was okay, but there were too many emotions

to properly fish with
if you have a concern
for catching verse. She preferred
the outdoors to living inside a
box, she decided. On the porch, deboning
a little poem she'd caught, thinking through
her life from the bothered surface
down, she found surcease

from care in looking at the trees
doing nothing, waving slightly, and
the nodding roses that grew two by two
by the porch. Further off were
lakeside flowers, *lacustrine*
lilies you'd call them, and water lapping.
Something glittered in the grass beyond the
gate. She found it was a carnelian tie-pin,

lost on some long-ago evening
by some long-gone gentleman, its
setting tarnished, the surface of the
carnelian clouded. Taking a turn
at twilight around the shore of the lake
she found she'd grown older, and turning to
a sound on the surface of the water

she noticed the image of the moon tossed
on the ripples, backward and forward,
seeming to be made up of flake on flake
of phosphorescent light. There, the
poem—its back browned,
its belly silver, tossed and shied in
to shore and—*there*—it was caught.

Paid Meridian

I had stretched out the silk
and I was just about to sketch the image of a fish—
no, not a fish, a bird, maybe a goose—
        some kind of bird
anyhow, when Joan rang. 'Have you heard?
we've moved into a new flat above a Thai
restaurant! Hey, Fred hit me in the eye
last night at that book party for Robert Duncan—
it was an accident, Fred sent me a note
this morning: "Sorry. I was listening to the drums."
Isn't he crazy? Come on over!' So here I am at Joan's
party, and the talk gets dirty,
it's one of those noisy events in a walk-up cold-
water flat with some music performance in the next room
        already,
it sounds 'experimental', but already
I'm on my way home on the uptown
        bus—
thanks very much—parties make me anxious, I get
faint and claustrophobic if it's too
noisy or too crowded, do you think people notice?

Besides I have no obligation—
stuck in a hallway—to chatter to some creep
or claque of enthusiasts. Outside it's—alas, alack—
a day for wearing a heavy coat
against the brown wind—
        if you're going out
in NYC the winter wind
sucks the avenues like a vacuum,
now, walking four blocks in just a jacket it
hits me like a freezer chilling the street.
All I want, really, is a clean, cosy loft,
instead I have to put up with some dank

cheap joint, rank
from the Korean cooking downstairs, blank
         walls, blank thought—
I pick up a pen—the phone rings, it's Joan: Hello?
Thanks for the party, Joan, but there's nobody here,
         really, nobody at all.

The Green Buick

'You remained for me a green Buick of sighs,
o Gladstone!'
—FRANK O'HARA, 'SECOND AVENUE'

I'm off, he said. He shrugged on a soft dark
overcoat, and wrapped a check scarf around his neck.
He stuffed his sighs into the Buick
ignoring the way the late afternoon cloud-light
glittered along the strips of chrome and gold trim.
A few spots of rain glistened on the metallic
lemon-green paint shine but somehow not on the
actual paint. What is it with the *New Yorker*, he said,
as he heaved his old suitcase into the back seat—
he had the white canvas top down,
the car was full of junk—that the writing
has to agree with the *faux-naïf* cover art,
as well as the advertisements for English raincoats
and cruises to the Bahamas? You'd think
one humiliation would be enough! Look at it,
he said. He looked around for the last time.
We're talking New York circa 1960,
the Apple just beginning to go
bad at the core. As for the San Fran-fucking-
Cisco Renaissance, he grunted,
the whole boatload of sensitive bullshit—
he thumped the flank of the car with his hand,
and it was like jolting a slide projector:
in his brain a magazine clunked to the right, then
slithered left, and dropped a fresh splash of colour
in the slot—he could see the Buick already swaying
over the wooden planks above the swollen river
and then down the track to his childhood home—
ah, the blue gloom under the trees, he said,
the neon burning outside the motel
in a halo of rain sparks—ecstasy!

Trastevere

God, here I am, hungover inside
the little café near the markets, jittery,
scribbling a babble of sentimental language
in my purple notebook emotion container—
no, buy some strawberries
(fruit market) in the sun
from the old Italian women
who mutter 'Thank you, signora, it's a pleasure
to serve even a rich and impious
Anglo lady such as yourself, take
another punnet, our brothers take precedence
in our father's will, but we're content
with that.' Now in the context
of the blues—oh yeh—
a love song about an owlet
or a moo-cowlet playing up
don't seem right. Under the clumsily-painted exit
sign an old lady sits shelling some freshly-picked
peas, delicious, piling them into a mound
on her lap. Her sister fills a large brown bowl
with blueberries and an arrangement
of little lilac petals. I wonder who
that is in the mirror, tossing her blonde curls. It
must be time for a drink—it is!
She dips the tip of her tongue
into her martini, and the repetition
of this gesture is her
way of saying hi, hi there, only
the pink tongue continues
to taste the gin, and she thinks
of those poor old women, not
bequeathed as much as the boys,
but old men's wills are carved
in granite. They were not articulate,

their clothes were black, their hair was grey.
No, not granite—Italian marble.
Memo—*Brush the dust off*
Emily's gravestone.
In back, the old brothers, each
wants to say something, but
each keeps it to himself.
The blueberries, all right, I'll take ten
punnets, thank you Signora Gamberoni—
sorry, Gamberi—no, two punnets, and
some salad stuff, there, under
the gas stove ad with the flame
painted the colour of tomatoes—oh, and ten
tomatoes, this instant!—
what am I saying?—sorry to ruffle
your feathers like that—be patent—
I mean patient—yes, I'd get sick of
tourists too, in your sensible shoes,
I don't know how you put up
with jerks like us, with our bovine yearning
for a clean bedroom, a fresh towel
every day, hot baths—don't you
love the way the gin—sorry, the
vino di fragola speaks of the terra
rossa soil that nurtured it?—wave
after wave of Americans, they think they own
the bloody planet. Maybe the extra sedative
I took last night—blemish
in the mirror—who's that blond
person looking sideways
at me, that gigolo look, as if
I was someone special—uh-uh, 'blond' disqualified
by a lack of the terminal gender indicator 'e'—
Perec's lipographic novel paints the modern city

as a sad arena for the hereafter
to fill with cruel laughter—
did you know that?—what a peculiar person
this blonde (click!) next to me is, with her
fake air of neutrality—
rhymes with sensual-ity—
different but equal sedatives—equalibrium—
what was her name
again? Tourists every—
where, they sit and scribble
in their mauve notebooks, equal
parts of prose and gush—lateral
thinking, please!—they go home with
some friend after the café's closed,
they stroll home, lips
brushing, brain like an eraser
that cancels the vapid entry in her
diary—waiter, another crème de ment—
sorry, 'menthe' is what I ment—meant—
just before I passed out
trying to remember the name
of that cute little thing
and that old Leonard Cohen song she sang
in the nightclub—she was a she,
all right, and she spun some line
about love, about how I was just as divine
as the moon in the heavens above,
blah, blah—now who
the fuck was she? Two by two,
hand in hand, my heart
beginning to pound
when she closed the bedroom door
behind us. What's that noise? Her pet cuckoo—
or was it an owl—owlet—activ-

reactive—chirping—what a pair, now
my heart begins to moo
like a lovesick cow. These
strawberries will do just fine, these
ones here. Hey, will you look at this?
No, not the vegetables, the *mirror*, honey—this
bustling vista full of tourists, this
couple just getting started on this
goofy voyage of learning—thank you—how this
shoulder is for you to lean your pretty head against.

Radium

It's just an empty room
in a beach house. You go
somewhere for drinks, stay out late,
get lost coming home. It's the awful page I
choose to look at in a diary, a challenge
like walking under a nest of hornets
to show I can do it. It's what draws
flame down from the sky, it
waits for me too, a sad delta
wasting and giving the sandy
water back to the greedy sea—look
closer—at the message the grass
has scribbled on the sand—then late at night, a hint of
a distant party like radium glowing
behind the horizon. Forget death. Indoors, a heap of rags
in a corner, paint-smudged clouts
of denim, one canvas shoe, a can of bleach
and a cheap notebook with all
the names of the
guests—*knock*
knock, it's the neighbour returning the oars
he's had since
last September, and
Janice, and the neighbour's kids—all
sunburnt—there's some ice blox in the
ice-box, all right? Only
now to lie on the bed of pine needles
and smell the iodine stink of seaweed
in the air, to trace on the rocks
that turn a cold shoulder to the turbulent water
the maps of lichen
each plotting an outline of a boulder
on the back of a boulder, only—it can't be quite
what it used to be, it can't be quite the same.

2

How much have I suppressed?
A career and a way of talking enfolding
a talent, like a tree and its shadow.
Not the shadow of a cut stump
blurred on an overcast
day when nothing
happens in the depths
of these woods, but a resonance,
a tiny scream
ascending
into the blue above the bay,
above the populated islands,
the cloud in its slow roil and tumble
spreading like gossip and persisting
into an evening of gentle rain.
In the morning, patches of bright
reflected blue cold
among the pine cones
beside the rubbish tip,
an icicle dripping a tear
of distilled water and fractured
brown rocks
tasselled with ice, these point
out to us what's passing:
a horrible clatter of wings.
There you are, in the snapshot, without
clothes, just a drape, a loose
swathe of something printed with ripe flowers
and knotted buds breathing around you, probably silk,
holding out a branch
dabbled with what looks like blood.

In Praise of Sandstone

Look at the rows of houses—no, not those ones,
    these ones, lit up by the morning sun chiefly,
look at the Botanical Gardens, the cabbage trees, the slopes
    of brownish grass, held up by the strata beneath.
An old bus negotiates a corner, with squeaking springs.
    There's a bank clerk, he gives a chuckle
as he passes the Water Police building and sees the carving
    of a soldier and a mermaid, meant perhaps to entertain
the passing workers. Think how stone has defined this region:
    dig anywhere, you'll find it in various places:
flanking the new expressway, it forms a flowing background
    for the traffic—hotel bars and coffee lounges
feature slabs of it—wall, floor—if you're doubting
    its ubiquity just look at the headlands that butt
head first into the Pacific, a hundred-mile outcrop
    of golden stone, tall breakwaters for the waters to
break on, protecting the city. Every local vineyard
    owner has to dig up blocks of it—I bet they wish
they'd chosen somewhere else for their grapes, but whether
    they like it or not, it's the short straw they must take.

Let's leave the present for a while, and dig down
    through the past, to more brutal times.
There's a team of convicts, half-heartedly engaged
    in hacking a hole in the rock to put a building in.
The overseer—that's the overseer, I think—
    though he's lashing into them, he seems unable
to establish to the satisfaction of all a superior moral
    position. The men stand, chained in a line,
mute and mutinous, and the red-faced shit responds
    by lashing them again. There's no sign of awe
in their demeanour, they know their position is fixed
    forever under the lash. Lush valleys

lie just over the ranges, there the natives are walking
        to and fro under the eucalypts—their cultural space
slowly shrinking—they don't know yet quite how unlucky
        their future will be—gathering nuts and fungi
and imaging that the ceremonial shapeliness of their lives
        will inspire the invaders to incline to common
decency, brotherhood, philanthropy and charitable works.
        Back in the present we see charity a pimp
to power, we hear how politics lacks a voice
        the people can understand, how it bullies all
but the best and the worst of us . . .
                    That is why, I suppose
        the city echoes a structure we've never sought
and hardly wish for, where threat is made external
        and inside the dim buildings a bureaucratic life
weaves its complex patterns. A government clerk wastes
        an afternoon singing, in a back room an accidental
discovery leads to a divorce, portraits of a dozen saints-to-be
        look down on rock samples and mineral gravels.
A little way outside the city, between two dull rivers
        lies the perfect setting for a tomb.
The sky is still, the khaki earth is silent, both
        rivers, too full for speech, turn their backs and
glide on to the sea. Is it far-fetched
        to imagine the strata of rock as the whisper,
layer on layer, of an ancient ocean's dream? Nothing
        remains of those creatures whose obscure love
sifted to sediment, then rock. Don't be sad
        at the thought of their extinction; in a way it's right
they should give up their tiny myriad lives for what looks
        like an endless beach solidified. A building site
is an absence of stone, time in a hollow running backward
        into the earth, then forward again, connected

to mankind's wish to make the future more certain
        by giving it the shape of a cave, though not quite
a cave, more a wish's projection in the air of itself
        flopped inside out and propped up like a question
to do with vanity, shelter and protection. Only a poet
        can know what they wanted, those tribes calling
across the empty plateau, their querulous uneasy
        articulation of immemorial fear and doubt.
A city is made up of more than urchins and gamins
        seething and quarrelling beneath a colonnade;
if the culture's old enough, it follows nature's
        pattern—veins of a leaf, arteries, what
gives life spreads out radially, citizens are caught
        in the processes, fed, recycled, until they resemble
their own parents tangled in the fight for food and water
        and a protected place in the sun. See these
city blocks made up of individuals, their music
        rising like skyscrapers, powerful though invisible,
shadowing the shape of the drive of the race forward
        into its own terrible and unwanted future. But if
we truly knew that the living are few and the dead
        are many, we'd wish in the end to be shaped into
cool squares, a courtyard full of shade, fountains
        and drains, a peaked roof rising to a point
with a steeple, supporting walls made from
        blocks of our own substance, with nothing of
the sea-creatures lives remembered in it, no love
        or fear to recall except the dreaming murmur
of a hive, a city, a sandstone landscape.

Chinese Poem, after Mark Ford

Christmas, Grandad came down from the mountains,
and we had to go fishing, on the ornamental lake.
The ornery mental lake, that's what I call it.
'Do I have to, Pop? It's just
animal death!' Fishing,
fishing, till everything is killed.
'How's the love-life?' Grandad asked.
My father was having trouble, some affair
that was going wrong. He shook his head.
'That's your karma,' Grandad opined,
'and moving house, that makes it worse.'
The waves rocked the boat, and it began to rain.
Grandad pulled on a pullover covered with marbled
patterns to resemble the surface of the water.
'Do you smoke dope? Never mind,' he said,
and popped a pill. 'Ahhh . . . that's better. Here's the trick:
you kill fish by not caring. But an old man
can only speak for himself.'

Christopher Brennan

He spoke German,
fluently, and French.
One he got by study,
the other from an inclination to drink
absinthe, like the poets who were always writing
among the cafés and the bottles and the crowds of women.

How do they do it? He liked women,
though they seemed a little too German,
at times, invading the domain of writing
and buggering up his whispered amatory French
the way that a few too many drinks
would ginger up but addle the study

of his volumes of foreign verse. In the study
he worked at a huge monument to women
for an hour or two, then had a drink.
Phew! Like a good German
he had a method for everything, and like the French
he wasted it on writing
poems about feeling like writing

all through the night. His study
lamp glowed out across the Quad. Famous French
poets wrote to him, once or twice. Women
from one end of Europe to the other admired his German
manners. Ah, Heidelberg! Must be time for a drink.
Back to the heatstruck colonies. God, a drink

would go down well, eh? Those oafs writing
gibberish and hoping for a pass in German
Romantic literature, look at them, as though study
were enough! What about inspiration? The women
of Sydney are not really suited to modern French

poetry. And now Mallarmé's gone loony—too French,
if that were possible. One last drink.
In a sheep-farming province, young women
who wish to develop the discipline of writing
should take up the study
of German . . .

He yearned to dream in French, but all he heard was German.
He inclined to drink, and trudged through a torrent of study
and when he reached for women, they became his writing.

Epitaphs

It seems so long ago—tell me, did you bring your family
to our marriage of convenience and regret? I remember
your hearty cousins fresh from the Home Counties, so
pleased with their good selves, ready to chance an arm,
their knack with spoon and needle an astonishment.
Didn't you find time for a quick shot of something
with the blokes? That one with a noticeable tic, that other
nodding and leaning on a stick, their brave future
shouted on the back of a toilet door?

I admit the first funeral was a fright, like
losing a finger in a kitchen appliance. As the clods
were shovelled in, a last drum solo thudding on the lid,
I thought I spied at the back of the straggling rabble
your old mates peering anxiously about. Could they
score, in this dismal field with thistles looking on?
Perhaps a snort behind the brick pissoir . . .
at the wake, propped up beside the urn,
their dopey equanimity was like an insult.

And when your father's daughter
graduated from the school of hard knocks,
tell me, did you ask your trembling addicts?
And did they come, shambling? And remember
the party for the famous writer, gallons of grog,
tubs of meat and garlic? Oh what a throng:
magnates and turds, princesses and prostitutes
in a storm of money, and howls from the microphone.
Of course you brought your mewling, puking pals,
indeed, we had to hark and listen to them
barking in the lavatory like rottweilers, then
donating their vomit.

And then another coffin—of course,
there had to be, it's only logical—
and so again they lurk and dawdle out the back,
imprisoned in their shabby discipline: thong,
candle, ecstasy.
No parson so tied to his parish, no
bookkeeper so enslaved to ranks of numerals
as they to their feeble creed, as you
to your bookish memorials.

Now dusk gathers and buses trundle
back to their depots, a whining machine
hosing down the gutters: you can hear the century
grinding towards midnight and the stroke of the clock.
Do invite your bony junkies, sheepish and shivering;
they will haunt the lawns, frail now, drooling,
their handshakes clammy, weeping for what's been lost:
one on crutches, one on his knees, the others shaking,
grinding their teeth and rehearsing your epitaphs.

See Rover Reach

Something's bothering the dog tonight—
the neighbour's pig, maybe—it's not fair
the way they feed that thing. Your hair, under the porch light,
it reminds me of Jenny, my long-ago one-night stand—
at least we thought it was a one-night stand—at Baffin Bay,
drinking vodka and pissing on the ice in the night-air!
And then there was the time on the 'Ocean Spray'—
some affair!—stranded miles from land.
You know, there's something about the crowd's roar
in Madison Square Garden, when the stripper's about to fling
her bra into the audience, and a guy—like Mark Strand,
say—catches it—then the good times begin.
It seems—*hey!*—the damn dog's going to bring
something—*hey!*—some mangled thing home in
its jaws! Listen, I gotta go, and when you gotta go . . .

[*Later*] . . . How about that time when Rover brought
home a chewed address book, and the casual flow
of talk and friendship with the neighbours ceased? We
couldn't guess, then, what it meant, we thought
Jim was loyal to Jenny—instead he was all at sea
with a dozen different women, and no faith
in any of them. Listen, are you sure
you want another highball? Your hair's all furled
across your back, and the new neighbours can hear
that grunting noise you make, above the roar
of the traffic, and the sound of your breath.

Only a parson, you said, would find it drear,
the vista from our back porch, the whole world
stoned on diesel fumes from the expressway. It's true!
Ugly? No, I'm glad we bought here—it only seems
ugly in the daylight. I have these bad dreams
about the neighbours—no, not the *new*

neighbours, Jim and *Jenny*—how we made light
of their marital troubles—bad dreams about the pain
our 'friendship' caused them, and the plane
tickets Rover ate so they missed their flight
out of town that last, long, lonely night.

Grover Leach

'Goodbye, old teacher . . . Goodbye,
Old Dog Tray.'
—JOHN ASHBERY, 'AND YOU KNOW'

1

It's Saturday, meet me tonight,
Grover said to a young lady at the State Fair—
meet me under the electric light
that burns in the sky over the hot dog stand
under the Ferris Wheel by the edge of the bay.
Let the farm slumber in the night-air,
let the corn nod under the spray
as the waves beat against the land.
Meet me where the mob's roar
drowns our laughter, and our mad fling
will magnetically excite each strand
of feeling in the crowd, and the Wheel will begin
to spin and spark like a dynamo, and bring
the wonderful twentieth century rolling in!

2

I remember long ago
the ocean regularly brought
to the bay an ancient tidal flow,
and fish were caught, that's what we
sought, as kids, and thought
about the 'Old Dog Tray' and the sea—
a tea tray painted in simple faith
with a picture of a dog on the shore,
his bushy tail furled
and his ears pricked to hear
beyond the waters' roar
a drowning farmer's breath.
For Grover, life on the farm had grown drear
and he learned to despise the modern world.
His wife left him, though his heart was true,
the farm failed, and that's why, it seems
old Grover waded in, and drowned his dreams.
And so the farm sleeps, waiting for a new
owner, and Rover waits too in that yellow light
that seems to paint the wet sand with pain
so it resembles a watery plain
where screaming seabirds dash their reflected flight
over the glitter of the State Fair, Saturday night.

Elegy i.m. M.J.

in memoriam Martin Johnston, 1947-90

Not the smoke from the truck driver's cigarette
wreathed with gold by the early morning sun,
a delicate arabesque of light and shade—
      he's unloading flagons of moselle,
      hock, white burgundy and claret
      in the driveway of the Toxteth Hotel—

Not the scent of meat hissing on the grill
at the Balkan—the tables are filling up—
early one evening somewhere in the seventies
as the shops along Oxford Street come alight,
buses winding through the traffic, and
      Nicholas puts up the Mickey Mouse poster
      in the window of Exiles Bookshop
      advertising a poetry reading—

Not the sound of his wife's voice—'Oh,
put out your bloody cigarette
and stop snoring!'—as she
      tucks the blanket in—late winter,
      the cat curled at the foot of the bed—

Not a tricky ploy with a bishop in the final moves
of a game that seems to have fallen into a pattern
remarkably similar to Botvinnik's closing tactics
in the 1949 Russian Chess Championship—don't you
      think?—the party still going at 4 a.m.,
      an old Miles Davis record on the gramophone,
      the ashtray spilling over—your move—

Not the pop! as the cork
comes out of a bottle of cold retsina—
    Malamatina brand, the green and yellow label
    picturing a little man drinking
    from a tilted glass, the rays of sunlight
    blazing down from a Mediterranean sky—

None of these things can now delight
Martin Johnston, his journey at last
written out in full, Sydney to Sydney, via
    Greece, love, alcohol
    and the art of poetry.

The Beach

You open your eyes and realise it's the morning of a summer's day in the inner western suburbs of Sydney, the sun already baking the bowl of sky. Here the pollution is heavier than in the centre of town—the sea breeze nudges the smog westwards through the day and into the evening as the lights come on, the evenings of trysts and hamburger smoke and hot cars, the nitrous oxides cooking in the heat and filtering through the lungs of the working classes in the new suburbs on the baking Cumberland Plain stretching towards the outback. You remember that Sydney and Los Angeles are similar the way a rubber stamp is an echo of its image, a coastal plain with an escarpment ten or twenty miles back from the on-shore breezes so that a bowl is formed with a lid of cold air sitting on top of the warm air

and the smog thick with suspended particles and diesel fumes and deadly gas is dumped on the plain right where the people live but the inhabitants laugh, they're happy to breathe the contaminated air that gives them health as well as sickness. And now we've caught the bus and we're moving east towards the coast, the sea, the Pacific, longing for a cool drink—the buses are blue and white now, the colours of the sky, but they used to be dull green and cream, matching the beach at the foot of the grassy park at Bronte, and made in England, but with the postmodern age Australians tilted toward the Teutonic and the people now go to work in buses made by *Mercedes Benz*, a name meant to recall the beautiful daughter of a diesel millionaire going to boarding school in Switzerland and having lots of expensive fun;

and now in a flash I remember my first meeting thirty years ago with Stephen Knight, then just a young man fresh from Oxford, in the broiling sun at Tamarama Beach—he lay on the sand in long sleeves, long pants, hat, socks and sandals stretched out in a patch of shade lordly and isolate among the satyrs and sybarites but in the fully-clothed potential of his one day being a professor, even then rolling over in his complicated mind the prolix chilly downhill teleology of Malory's *Le Morte D'Arthur* towards armour-plated death,

so here we are, way back then, a couple of teachers, six young students, a bottle of Pernod, Ferdinand de Saussure and all, dozing and reeling around on the fabulous littoral, the mythological beach—

Hi, Stephen—well at least at an exemplar, one unit selected from the Venn diagram of the immense conceptual set of all the overlapping permutations and combinations of the poems, songs, articles and stories about where the shore meets the sea, and the actual twenty-seven foam-scalloped beaches that bedeck and embroider that doorstep of the South Pacific, Sydney.

~

The bowl of sand and water is a kind of memory theatre now: when I was a boy in the country I liked to swim, poke at an octopus with a stick and chase poisonous puffer fish through the rippling shallows, then I would wander up the five-mile beach, no one there, squinting against the light reflected from the white sand, a sack over my shoulder, collecting bleached cuttlefish bones to sell to the store for bird feed—another time walking along a ridge of grassy sand where the hollows are full of heat and stillness, I trod on a snake with my bare feet and got such a fright I didn't think to snap shut the shotgun and shoot. Now the beach seems a tedious gritty way to get skin cancer—just as when I was a kid in a country town I longed to live in Australia's busiest metropolis, Sydney, and once I got there and failed a few university courses and worked at the Orange Spot Bar midnight till dawn selling the prostitutes fruit-cake sandwiches and mopping the floor, so I travelled, but found London was no better, Iran at least had crystal fresh air

but nowhere to swim let alone a beach,

and in Afghanistan the bell-boy sold you dope for a dollar a handful, but the police threw you in jail if they found you with an alcoholic drink—

why are we always restlessly searching for a way to help us avoid thinking about the final payment to this charade, death?

In the end, sad joke, it's the wages of fun.

~

Let's turn back to the landscape—not the real one, this one, which is just a work of art, like something sketched with a pencil and then painted onto a large sheet of paper with those grainy water-colours, the paper crinkling where it's wet—in one sense every artist is just a magnified version of a kid having fun—

but of course there's more to it, namely meaning and characters— once on the radio I heard the art critic Peter Fuller say in his serious English voice 'of course, some landscapes are more meaningful than others', and I laughed so hard I hurt a muscle in my jaw and had to go to the doctor—everyone knows the meaning gets stirred in at the last minute the same way you add mould inhibitor to a can of bathroom paint! and as for characters, just look around you—not at the painted paper, look at Sydney sliding past outside the bus window glittering with shops and traffic and its freight of noise and activity, Vietnamese immigrants, here's an Italian family quarrelling, and a Greek fish shop crowded with revellers in white—there seems to be a wedding celebration going on, and the bride's father is yelling at the groom—more characters than you can poke a stick at, every one of them slowly and inexorably heading towards a common end, that unwilling emigration from the country of the living to join the multi-million population of the land of death—

so our feelings write themselves onto the view, turning geography into landscape, distorting the weather. Imagine a sleepy romantic picnic under the trees brought to an embarrassed end with a flurry of leaves and the first pattering drops then the bruised, boiling clouds occupy the sky and a cold rain darkens and fills the summer air

with chill electricity—so we inscribe our feelings onto the backdrop, if a landscape is really a backdrop, the way a young guy in love might notice when he lifts his drink

that it leaves a ring of moisture on the surface of the table and he absent-mindedly traces out a word with his fingertip—a name—seven letters that are full of magic for him, but not for anyone else in the darkened bar, they're just tired from their day at the beach.

~

It seems to take ages to get to the coast from almost anywhere, so perhaps we should forget the bus and take the car instead and just put up with the fact that there's nowhere to park and the acres of boiling hot macadam burn the soles of your feet, and when you finally arrive at Bondi Beach you trudge along the famous golden sand spiked with rusty needles soaked with hepatitis and HIV and junkie spit wondering what the 'style' of the place really represents—you notice the Esplanade is crowded with Japanese brides getting their wedding cheap—they say in Tokyo it costs a fortune with all the presents for the thousands of guests including every fellow worker and all the superiors from the office and their wives, so it's less expensive to fly to Sydney and have the ceremony at the Nippon International and send everyone back home a video—they stroll past the old milk bar that sells Chiko rolls, milkshakes and fizzy drinks, looking for a sushi bar or maybe an American nightclub and trying to get that casual Australian slope into their walk which has been stiffened by a lifetime of restrained competitive frenzy in Tokyo or Yokohama, they walk right by Martin Smith's bookshop and never think to drop in and chat and maybe ask for a bit of light reading . . . nothing too demanding, you know what I mean, something gushy and fake like *The Piano*, say, to pass the time—their honeymoon time—or a book of haiku about Australian native animals—*ha, Aussie Haiku! Excellent!*—about native animals, right, but not the ones that creep up inside your trouser-leg and sting and kill, and not the nightmare creatures, say the shark as big as a refrigerator that scoops your thigh off in the blink of an eye and you don't feel it for a few seconds, then you feel it, and see the spreading red cloud—surely savage predators wouldn't live anywhere near such a crowded beach

and in any case we can see the surf lifesavers patrolling in their kindergarten-coloured caps and costumes and the poles topped with flapping pennants that spell out the difference between safety and danger more bluntly than the social rules that say you can go just so far with a girl but no further, cravats are in but safari jackets are definitely out this year, and shorts and thongs are not allowed in the Jungle Bar—and a team of hefty lads are dragging a boat into the water, a large elegant rowing boat with half a dozen oars, then they butt through the first wave, the nose lifting up then thudding down onto the water again, it seems to be fun

but it's really a serious kind of work that gives out a noble and metallic social aura because the young men are all volunteers—so are the bush fire fighters with their tankers of life-saving water— here it's the water that kills—and in both cases it's youth facing down the unimaginable that can strike us anywhere and—we hope— defeating it with their strength and guts—you feel a glow of grati- tude towards them and plan to shout them all a drink

at the clubhouse afterwards but a gesture like that could be badly misinterpreted, and you notice—as the nose of the boat heaves up into the air again—that some of their costumes are very skimpy, if that's the right word, disappearing into that cleft between the buttocks as the helmsman leans on his oar half-submerged in a boil- ing green turmoil, the other oars waving in the spray like the feel- ers of a giant praying mantis—they wouldn't allow that kind of exhibitionism in Melbourne but hey, this is Sydney,

right? And anything goes—the boat smashes down onto the back of the wave—you duck as a chopper roars over the crowd from some- where behind the beach and whistles out to sea, rotors flailing the air and beating the surface to a creamy froth that leaves a lacy pattern of foam as though a huge doily was racing over the water,

flying on a mission to protect the eastern flanks of the city from ever-present death.

≈

It's hard to imagine that dark force reaching up and taking you in daylight under the glaring blue sky, death

belongs to midnight and silence, to the long quiet end of things, to shadowy corridors and empty rooms, to the hospital ward where my father's life leaked away, the starched sheets where my mother's tiny body lay curled in the gloom like a child's, the polished lino floor of the kitchen where my uncle Martin pitched forward and fell, surprised, and in the silence heard his poor battered heart stumble to a stop—it doesn't belong with us gathered here on the sunny crowded beach

with the cries of children and the tinkle of the ice-cream van a few blocks away and the squawk of seagulls filling the windy air.

But death doesn't answer our queries, it doesn't bother laughing at us. It sneaks in with the morning breeze, it mixes with the smell of burnt sausages at the family barbecue, with the hiss of gas escaping from a keg of beer, it blends with the chlorine crystals filtering to the bottom of the municipal swimming pool, it blinks in time to the fairy lights and bounces along with the party balloons and the fun

at Mardi Gras and it washes into the gutters that drain the streets of Sydney

and down the sewers into the Harbour and out to the Pacific, a spreading stain, it takes your friends and your enemies alike, and in the middle of the good times it tugs your sleeve and murmurs to you whether you want to listen or not. One summer evening when I tilted into Martin's Bar on Oxford Street—this must be twenty years ago—and asked for a drink

~

the topless waitress—her pretty tits tipped with pink lipstick wobbling in time to the disco music pumping from the speakers— she asked 'What kind of drink? We've got hundreds,' and I said 'How about a martini?' and she blinked and said: 'Martini, ahh . . . I know, that's the one with the *olive*, right? Sorry, pet, we're out of olives, how about a strawberry, okay?' I said 'Are you kidding? A *strawberry*? Just give me a drink

of gin with a dash of dry vermouth, please, no strawberries.' And in the shadows a ghost touched my shoulder and whispered in my ear 'Hey, have you tried this? It's better than drink. Friends of yours have gone to sleep in its arms. How about a shot of death?'

No, no thanks, no death. In Sydney

let's say there's no more dying, each word we speak holds it at bay for one more minute, and where there's a party there's music and happiness, so no dying on and beyond and behind the beach

and in the sloping layers of rented rooms and apartments that stretch uphill, a tilting layer cake made of brick and tile behind Bondi glimmering in the twilight and pulsing with life, under the shade of the trees in the empty avenues, the cars asleep under the street lamps that swap glare and shadow, shadow and glare, you hear the shuffle of stealthy footsteps, clink of a bottle, happy whispering, but no sadness, just a perplexed and sometimes tiring kind of fun,

okay?—just fun, don't ask questions—in the warm air.

∼

So quick, drop your book, get a drink, breathe in the air
and laugh at death. Under the bright blue canopy it's time for fun;
it's a summer's day in Sydney, and everyone's going to the beach.

Five Modern Myths

The Guarani Indians of Paraguay
like to keep a small cork loose in their dishwashers,
to 'introduce a spirit of lightness and unpredictability
into what is otherwise a repetitive activity,
and one tedious and unpleasant to contemplate
by the gods of the forest.'

In Kota Rendang, a small fishing village
on the east coast of Malaysia, the wood carvers
refrain from spitting in front of the local cinema
'in case Clint Eastwood should become angry,
and blunt the edges of our blades.'

Until recently the fishermen of Muckle Roe,
in Scotland, used to scrub their decks with toothpaste
on the night of the Summer Solstice,
in order to placate the fish-goddess Fiona,
she 'of the gleaming teeth'.

The Mongolians of Ulaanbaatar have a great respect
for dwarfs, who are trained to recite poetry
in a sing-song voice in front of the television news
which is allowed to run silently in the background.
'A short rhyme contains the news', is their motto;
using 'contains' in the sense of 'constrains', or
'keeps within the bounds of propriety'.

The stockbrokers of Lakeville, Connecticut,
take care not to be seen mowing their lawns
on the thirteenth of the month, in case
a water spirit, the 'White Witch of Lakeville',
should afflict them with cirrhosis of the liver.

Three Poems about Kenneth Koch

1

He never writes poems about writing poems,
this dog-eared wunderkind who's tapped
the unconscious of the race. His main characteristics:
in the fall he develops a fatal liking for stiff gin
martinis. He's not a disguised Mayor Ed Koch—
the hair's different—and don't let anybody tell you
he is. He kisses wives under the mistletoe,
given half a chance, and he's a sink of indiscretion,
so look out, gossip-wise. A knot of contradictions, he is
a simpering tough guy, and a brutal sook—mercy me,
here he comes! Violently athirst!

2

There's a book of Tasmanian verse titled *Under Aldebaran*,
but it isn't Kenneth's, thank goodness. On the street
where he lives he'll grin down from his window at you,
and if he borrows a domestic pet he'll give it back
pronto. Wait a minute—I think
I said 'gin martinis' when I meant 'beer
and pretzels.' Unhh . . . songs about old
dogs and whisky drunkards make him cry all day—
the neighbours chuckle indulgently, and they never mind.
A young woman student cries 'Oh, Kenneth!
Will you *stop* that?' and slaps him. He does try, but
he has blood in his veins, he's not dead
in the pants like some old professor with only one thing—
nuclear physics, say—on his mind. He's travelled the world
until he's weary, and he's been to a thousand World Series
games. He thinks constantly on the greatness
of Edna St Vincent Millay. He's quietly proud
of his conversational Greek, and one time
he gobbled a whole bag of bagels in Dinky's Delicatessen.

3

Pondering the Orientations of Kenneth, we are
wondering if Chinese restaurants are not
unknown to this gentleman. He steps
jauntily to the mirror, his reflected youthfulness
dazzling the other diners and the waitresses too.
Now he writes a poem, and garnishes it with a colon!
He leaves for Mexico, and, once there, decides to vanish—
a pop, a flash, and a small, perfectly-formed miasma
has entirely replaced him.
Grieving this deprivation, the skies are overcast.
'Señor Coke's poems, ever shall we recite them!'
sob the local chaperones. From, say, sere Tamazunchale—
no, from the shopping malls of steamy Miami
to the brothels of bourbon-dark Jacksonville
a draught of Koch is known as a certain cure
for flabby verse—certain, though bitter. He argues with Jews
about God, and vice versa, dispersing and hiding
his subtle talent in the libraries of Philadelphia
until the police under their blathering sirens become depressed
at the thought of the loss of the illuminations of Kenneth.

Black Sugar

This is her best dream, isn't it pathetic?
To go to France and study for years, to learn
how to be fucked in the head convincingly.
His eyes were like a dark green passport

to study in France for years to learn
a high, serious, ashamed way of eating a salad.
His eyes were like a dark green passport—
Take that! and I woke, I felt hot.

A high, serious, ashamed way of eating a salad.
Oh yes, he pulled back from the bed, saying
Take that! and I woke, I felt hot. Julia
was clambering out of orgasm, her lips wet.

Oh yes, he pulled back from the bed, saying
I lost her! I dived at my fate: Julia
was clambering out of orgasm, her lips wet,
but I guess to her it's just business.

I lost her, I dived at my fate,
sucking money out of the capitalist system:
I guess to her it's just business.
How to get a degree in black sugar jazz,

sucking money out of the capitalist system—
it's grotesque: all she wants to learn
is how to get a degree in black sugar jazz,
in French, and to handle nostalgia well.

It's grotesque, what she wants: to learn
how to be fucked in the head convincingly
in French, and to handle 'nostalgia' well;
this is her best dream, isn't it pathetic?

The New Season's Patterns

The new season's patterns shocked everybody
and made a name for the brash young designer:
with a motif of orchid doodles and cobalt zips.
Deftly moving chilled beer from fridge to freezer

made a name for the brash young designer.
From navy Miami for example, to puce shock towels,
deftly moving chilled beer from fridge to freezer
to the click of his bossy business.

From navy Miami for example, to puce shock towels,
meandering moodily among the midget factions
to the click of his bossy business.
Among the rubble, a weathered velocity

meandering moodily among the midget factions
gives the trade away: abandon the machine.
Among the rubble, a weathered velocity,
and she seemed head over heels in love with me.

Give the trade away. Abandon the machine.
But then it went wrong, and I can't—couldn't—
and she seemed head over heels in love with me,
so I sorted out the essence of what tied me to her—

but then it went wrong, and I can't—couldn't—
I'd gone crazy about her and they had to sedate me,
so I sorted out the essence of what tied me to her.
The rows of bungalows in the moonlight—

I'd gone crazy about her and they had to sedate me
with motifs of orchid doodles and cobalt zips.
Rows of bungalows in the moonlight:
the new season's patterns shocked everybody.

Like Advertising

Like advertising, and like hunger
the change lay gaping on the tray,
waiting for the waiter to make sense of it
and leaving a general blue fudge in the air.

The change lay gaping on the tray,
that's what we're still puzzling over.
Leaving a general blue fudge in the air
pieces of grit, cloud detritus, little sparkles—

that's what we're still puzzling over—
roared low over the damp fields and highways.
Pieces of grit, cloud detritus, little sparkles,
the sonic boom as his immense talent

roared low over the damp fields and highways
thrilled some viewers. But it frightened others,
the sonic boom as his immense talent
blew up and ruined his reputation,

thrilling some viewers. But it frightened others.
Now I live with it. That damaged ego
blew up and ruined his reputation.
Damp, half-eaten sandwiches. Why?

Now I live with it, that damaged ego,
and now I regret I ever came back.
Damp, half-eaten sandwiches. Why?
Two stainless-steel cars glinted in the sun

and now I regret I ever came back
and waited for the waiter to make sense of it.
Two stainless-steel cars glinted in the sun
like advertising, and like hunger.

Rimbaud in Sydney

Romanticism has never been properly judged—
it is as simple as a phrase of music.
We grappled and triumphed over the subway map.
What the fuck is going on around here?

It is as simple as a phrase of music,
when you are seventeen. You aren't really serious:
What the fuck is going on around here?
I'm a fiery passionate woman—I'm not a raving loony.

When you are seventeen you aren't really serious.
Reality being too thorny for my great personality,
I'm a fiery passionate woman. I'm not a raving loony;
I chose to remain silent, reality

being too thorny for my great personality.
She paid for the operation with her own money:
I chose to remain silent.
Driven into harmonic ecstasy

she paid for the operation with her own money
with a butter knife in one hand and a Coke
in the other. Driven into harmonic ecstasy,
here I am: 'I've got enough money!'

With a butter knife in one hand and a Coke in the other
let us hear the confession of a companion in Hell.
'Here I am. I've got enough money.
It has been found again.' What? 'Eternity.'

Let us hear the confession of a companion in Hell:
'We grappled and triumphed over the subway map
until it was found again.' What? Eternity:
Romanticism has never been properly judged.

The Waiting Room

The movement slows: everything grows dark.
A man checks the knot in his tie. It's twilight
and a fine rain smears the windows.
Will you miss your train, and the delightful party?

A man checks the knot in his tie. It's twilight;
superhuman powers will never be yours.
You will miss your train, and the delightful party.
They argue about civil rights. At the checkout

superhuman powers will never be yours.
Reading the college diploma, looking for mistakes,
they argue about civil rights, at the checkout,
and some new psychiatric theory.

Reading the college diploma, looking for mistakes,
the shadows who dream of obscurity
and some new psychiatric theory
fade away. Why don't you look at that:

the shadows who dream of obscurity?
Well, there's always a first time for a thief.
Fade away, why don't you? Look at that,
a stumble, and the valuable vase gets broken—

well, there's always a first time for a thief.
Look, here comes the rich old fool. He smiles—
a stumble, and the valuable vase gets broken.
Far away in Chicago, the stock market rallies.

Look, here comes the rich old fool. He smiles,
and a fine rain smears the windows.
Far away in Chicago, the stock market rallies.
The movement slows: everything grows dark.

Amulet

Swimming in my memory, a place of pleasure
like a happy ending drifting through a dream.
She's on with a pale, plump guy, a walking migraine.
We heard her thrilled gasps on the TV news.

Like a happy ending drifting through a dream
this engraved amulet is a symbol of a tableau
on the TV news. We heard her thrilled gasps:
a girl buying a ring for the first time.

This engraved amulet is a symbol of a tableau
where her high-school friends are gathered.
A girl buying a ring for the first time,
I try not to get sentimental about her

when her high-school friends gather,
chattering in the kitchen. Touching hands,
I try not to get sentimental about her.
There was a globe that glowed when you lit it.

Chattering in the kitchen, touching hands,
a mournful song playing on the old radio.
There was a globe that glowed when you lit it
like a face grinning at a laughing child,

and a mournful song playing on the old radio.
She seemed to be reading, posed on the sofa
like a face grinning at the laughing child
dependent on pills—a book about a European city

she seemed to be reading, posed on the sofa
with a pale, plump guy, a walking migraine,
dependent on pills—a book about a European city
swimming in my memory, a place of pleasure.

The Seasons—Spring

Jack carefully lowered the needle onto the surface of the spinning vinyl. From somewhere out back came the sound: the Miles Davis quartet playing 'Autumn Leaves'. It was ages before the track got going—some drum doodle—then it took off like a rocket. But they were dead now, Jack reckoned. Susie had borrowed a red and white check jacket that suited the period, late forties. Jack had brought a rubber turkey, Dinky had invested in a hollow pumpkin with a candle inside. They went through the motions, mouthing the great playwright's words, while a bushel of copper-toned foliage cascaded over their shoulders and whirled around their feet. Maybe if they wished hard enough, Jack thought to himself, maybe they would find themselves seated around a little table out the front of the Café de Flore in—say—September 1953, drinking black coffee and green Chartreuse, laughing and arguing about whether Susie should have flirted with that writer at the publisher's party the night before. *Of course she should!* Then the audience went quiet, and the lights dimmed. Ah, how lovely! How rare the bubbles of air, wobbling up to the blue ceiling!

> *A baby sparrow*
> *falls to the footpath outside*
> *'Dirty Girls Revue'.*

The Seasons—Summer

Rodney twined a length of tartan ribbon around the sleigh bells on the reindeer's collar and paused, rubbing his stomach. Why had he ordered a second dozen at the Oyster Bar? He was developing a paunch. The staff had free access to the gym on Tuesdays; why didn't he use it? Tartan—some people call it 'plaid'. And they call plaits 'braids', and they call braid . . . That new junior—what was his name? Brad? Chad? He kept himself trim, all right. Tod, that was it! Tod had sipped his chilled frontignac, the glass beaded with moisture, Tod had traced a heart with his fingertip, Tod had glanced at Rodney across the oyster shells with a promise in his eyes—smoky grey eyes, with a glow of blue in the depths. But if he'd flirt with me—Rodney smoothed his toupee—if he'd have me, he'd have anybody, and who wants a slut like that? He felt his mouth pulling down at the corners. *I do, that's who.* He looked out through the plate glass, past the streams of pedestrians. Hyde Park was busy with Christmas shoppers. Wrappers and newspapers blew around their feet. There were lots of Japanese among the crowd, he noticed with pleasure, eating hot dogs and licking ice-cream cones. One old oriental gentleman, his forehead shaded from the fierce sun by a golf cap, was holding up a scrap of paper and reading something he'd written on it to a lady, probably his wife:

> *On the path, a snake*
> *fast asleep. High on a branch*
> *a shy morsel sings.*

The Seasons—Autumn

The flowers wilted under the studio lights, and Jerry sweated. His client, the Tokyo Girl Suspenders, wanted the freshest flowers, the juiciest leaves. He ran around with a little spray can of green paint and a copy of the *TLS*, touching things up. The Polaroids were awful—the emulsion had gone stale, and the model had some disease that made her skin go funny in the heat . . . whose voice was that, on the answering machine? Kathy? Uh . . . look, boss, the crop's coming on fine, the little tips are breaking through the soil of the solarium even as we speak. No one has ever managed to grow coca plants in Hackensack before . . . now spinning down into the void . . . no, not Tuesday, Bruno's doing me a new version of the script, in the first draft the guy dies of a stroke or something, it takes ages, I ask you, who is going to pay good money to watch some old fuck take an hour to die . . . now looking out the window so intently that you seem to shoot forward through the glass into the warm air high above the noise of traffic and out over the river . . . no, Proust he ain't. No, no Ode to Spring, no Rose is a Rose, no nothing. Say hullo to Harry for me. Hey, sweetheart, could you lay those Polaroids out under the sun lamp for five minutes?

> *The scotch melts its ice.*
> *Sunset on snow: eiderdowns*
> *aflame in the street.*

The Seasons—Winter

You look for that new Country & Western station at the Uptown end of the dial, hunting through the ads for hair cream and Japanese motor scooters. One. Homer describes the Shield of Achilles in Book Eighteen of the *Iliad*. Two. Alexander Pope translates Homer into English. Many years later, an ambitious souvenir wholesaler orders five gross of tiny bronze shields modelled on the frontispiece in the first edition of Pope's translation of Homer, an engraving of the Shield of Achilles, then we hear a short radio feature about a crowd filing through a museum in Madrid, the air conditioner on the blink, everyone perspiring horribly. While the tour guide describes the piece in front of them—a bronze reconstruction of a shield from the period of the Roman Republic made to the design given in Pope's translation of Homer—in a mixture of Spanish and English, the tourists notice that they are reflected in the polished nickel plating, drops of sweat and all. An old Scottish woman sees herself as a young bride, a retired used-car dealer from Normal, Illinois sees himself as his own son, and so forth. They begin to cry, one by one. The guide looks at them and shakes his head. This always happens. You switch off the mantel radio and glance out the window at the drift of brown smog that hangs over Sydney Harbour and casts a dirty veil over the Opera House, where you have an appointment at eight.

> *Dark falls early. Grim*
> *brokers hurry home to the*
> *close of the tax year.*

Uncollected Poems 1985–2000

Small Animal Poem

Okay, there's room for one
more small animal in my life,
behind the bad future, as long as he
doesn't complain. His fate will be secret;
      I am not to blame.

If you imagine you are not so
lucky today, rehearses the other,
the guilty animal, look at tomorrow—
the good days are gone, in future everything
      you do goes wrong,

you will be broken down. But
the new arrival, the blameless
animal, I warn him, is not to know
that his future's just begun, nor how soon
      the damage will be done.

The White Hole Paradox

for Martin Johnston

Like Chuang Tzu's logic lepidoptery the problem jumps
through the Black Hole and persuades us to think of it:
drifting up over the coffee horizon the poet wonders
'Would it be a worthwhile problem to write a poem
containing the words *psychopannychy* and *wayzgoose?*'
Writhing in a fit of *sortes virgilianae*
I open Proust for the first time in my life
and stumble on a phrase that skewers Doctor Leavis
and leaves him crushed, thin, flat and oblong,
a Doctor of Letters achieving the proper apotheosis of
turning into a bookmark nobody notices. The neighbors
act suburban, as they should; hammer blows on tin
rain down on the sun-struck acres of brick:
'The whole bloody wall's full of books!' and 'Look,
how's this—a hippy printer on a picnic drops acid
and gets hit by a truck! See? Psychopannychy!'
But the coffee grounds settle on the silted glaze,
the monk's bicycle moons and glitters in the hallway.
The problem waits around for its heroes; e.g. Li Po
would dash it off before his breakfast shot of booze,
then tear it up! Or, better still, Tu Fu thinks about
a complex structural form that would allow the entry
of both words, in Chinese, written by his friend Li Po
before breakfast on a napkin then folded into a
paper boat ('frail butterfly', don't forget Rimbaud)
and launched onto an autumn pond . . . like peach blossoms,
human hopes, et cetera . . . but the problem eludes us,
it seems further away than the Perfect Carburettor
(John Forbes) and though we think desperately we know,
in this poem at least, that it can't be done.

Two Haikus

Yeats at Bondi

Bondi Beach—
that drongo-thronged, that
nong-tormented sea.

Hawaiian Haiku

In Honolulu
nobody watches
Hawai'i Five-O'.

Two Short Poems, after Li Po

If you were to ask me why I dwell among green mountains
I should laugh silently. My heart is serene.
The peach blossom follows the moving water.
There is another heaven and earth beyond this world of men.

—LI PO (LI BAI)

1

In a small town in the Southern Hemisphere
a booze-up gets rolling at the RSL.
Why do I live here, in the Blue Mountains?
Ho hum, another Valium.
A disc jockey follows the moving waiter.
There is another cocktail bar outside
the liquor limits, and an American actor
asleep in the projection room.

2

Why do I think of Li Po staring
at the moon's reflection in the stream?
I'm laughing behind the plate glass,
quite sedated. Look, the shaving lather
follows the moving water.
Here, in Dullsville, New South Wales,
there is a heaven like a movie palace
and an academic asleep in the foyer.
On his lap, *What Bird Is That?*

Two Poems for Mr Stevens

1

I was of two minds,
like a hotel room
in which there are two people.

2

I do not know which I prefer,
the beauty of inflections
or the beauty of innuendoes,
her brief glance through the crowd,
or her looking-away.

What Mortal End

(as 'Tom Haltwarden')

Those quick inventive brains, who with early distant
Northern straits and naked shocks begin,
And the energy of the mossy barns, and children,
Who wait like us unblest. And there, at the mass
Of sad experience, thou art gone
Though sometimes seen among the fields and
Half-reaped fields would seem some quiet place
To lie before their smoked and turbid ebb
And stand, baffled by English hills where they
The inmost scholar on the hot race muses.
Wheatfields and flocks are eloquent, like other joy,
The long dewy grasses fresh in autumn,
Come on summer every human breast. For us,
If even lovers pine, with dew, or hanging pasture
Spark from the moon-blanched arts, our lips
Unchained thy hope. And well-nigh keep from heaven
And a distant boy, and scholar poor,
Our wisest an immortal lot, but none pursue.

From the dying pastoral slopes an unwanted earth art gone
And the vast edges draw back the impulse of an hour—
Exhausted, thou waitest for one desire, and the soft
Abstractions of reapers in the intellectual trough.
So wild brother men, concealed then with distracted air—
Let it be spent on other joy, and we,
Wanderer one of antique shadow, rest
And in the bluebell-drenched days, men
Who in the sun, thy fire their being roll.
Come, shepherd, bathe in our war of antique shadow,
'Tis this story of the wooden bridge, wrapt in disguise.

With that the vast edges draw back his genuine self,
The mystery of the winding murmur hearing
In this face, the grass where I am laid—when
The mystery of the tale begin again, and cease,
And dogs in all the unregarded bales.

Her Shy Banjo

(as 'Joy H. Breshan')

Rain, without it there can be no September music
The concealed afternoons
A source of the revisions as useless as a lukewarm fancy,
Making pink smudges on life and accepting severe punishment,
Encouragement by lovers, sang no more blades of light
Arise, light! The things of the day we eat
Breakfast each in their tree withdrawals,
Our marionette-like Pierrot, like these
Hot sticky evenings, though fragmented

The greatest risk working deep crevices far inland,
We can see no reward, winnowers of the old time
Involved without pain, with their sleepy empty nets
And you, at twilight.
The neighbours love the yellow of the same tweed jacket.
It is only semi-bizarre where you want to lie,
A nice, bluish slate-gray. People laugh,
Having conspired with a towel, and wiped the last thought
From the black carriages, the models slender, like the stars.
You couldn't deliberately, for fright, once you see
It's all talk, the travelling far from anybody.
Hands streaming with kisses, between us.
It may be something like silver,
Something like a sponge, and they enjoyed it, abandonment
Without shame, a crowded highway in the sun, it just
Stays like dust—that's the nature of the children, and
Yesterday's newspapers say: 'Sometimes good times follow bad.'
Their object, the sky. Is it like climbing abruptly
From a room? It may be only a polite puss-in-boots we passed,
Two in love hesitant at the front door.

So we have enjoyed the one crisp feeling, raking
And breathing, checking the horrible speech the furniture
        makes.
How short the season is—don't fix it if it comes in coloured
Mottoes, and now, underneath this dilemma directly, as
Our clothes, the afternoon, really old-time, her shy banjo.

Fin de Siècle

Families of seething photons boil off the TV screen,
one movie after another rocketing to their apotheosis,
reel after reel stuffed with plots and characters.

Plausibly chockablock with passion, equally
helpless with a boil of anger, blooming
into a fidgety sketch of the century we
leave—what's it done for us?—just
in time for the second feature, how
perfect in its glazed replication of film noir!

Maybe history is really a Morals Calculator
endlessly looping through its revelations, time
after time: War, Jazz, Killing, the dwarfish dark gods
damned if they'll let us go until we learn the lesson.

New Poems: The Malley Variations

An American in Paris

A beautiful nap, and April comes to kiss
my bleak mood. We have sunlight, at last.
Paris drags itself into spring,

a moist pink glow in the ashy sky.
I drift to the party. I sing black, then white,
I have I found you, my brothel,

my next mirage. A woman gets up wearily,
bulging and superb. She at the wash basin . . .
I might pollute her, the humblest mortal alive

melancholy with perspiration.
A businessman enters, he takes off his jacket.
Red wine, dandruff, gaudy socks,

a foul faithfulness. And yet I know
why she is warming his fingers.
He has a poem in his pocket. They read, and,

chock-full of looking, make a speech:
the artist needs loneliness. Always
alone—Walt Whitman, Poe.

My blood falters. Loneliness? Memo:
Speak to God in private. A noise outside—
the president of the planet, in the dark street?

It must be Him. His hands are buildings.
I return to the pool of contempt.
I write. I write what? *Mélodie*

d'amour: the room is lined with books
and the next play will open the shutters
on a very epic of devotion.

Benzedrine

Love is endless oil and the best
robots doze in jail, waiting
for the roof-vibrating voice,
the chatter on the streets more piercing
than a princess screaming under a meat truck.
My trembling ass will sit on her brilliant eyes.

Yet in my pocket I keep a fortune cookie:
'Frictions lead nowhere, vinegary death.'
I have been bitter with you, I have
waited in dreams and invented
the twenty-five thousand comrades
who came to resurrect the tubercular utterance
from the fading vomiting wave, each heart
a package devoured by the cannibal dynamo
of corporate growth.

And from the narcotic haze of Bloomingdale's
I was that damaged old man who watched
the inept shoppers mount a ladder of pain,
debtors who copulated with the cash economy
and were burned alive in the money vortex
despite the interpolations of intelligent editors,
those human prose angels who night after night
traced a pencil across a screen.

You lived with articulate migraines
where the Chinaman of the Southern Shore
cavorted in a sideshow; mustard-gas girls appear
in the divine aquaria where you drink,
and the moist, gaunt waitresses of advertising.

You will be that charm whom I abandon,
wake up in poverty and then, in disgust, return to,
upon my tongue the spittle of insulin.

The Master of the Black Stones

The master listened, a vacant expression
on his face. Would this be his last game?
I was worried that the amateur audience
would be sickened by the violence of the conflict.
The planets symbolised the different openings
and the weather was a problem, ever since
his tournament among the foreigners to the east.
The clock was a good persuader.

Aeons of crisis, then we see the incredible patterns
that he was fond of spreading across the board.
'And I must go among rage, envy and ugly rumours,'
he complained. 'Roses, perfumes, idylls breathed
in my travels, dying upon the sad autumn of my age.'
He had endured pain and the slant sun
descending behind the abraded hill.

Now he saw the four naked breasts of his two wives
as they hovered near in the dim evening light.
His first wife, what was her mountain girlhood like?
Angels lighting a teacher. I looked
in her hand for the line of shadows
and obscurity, playing on a sofa
by the night's other darkness.
Therefore the goat's horn, the white flowers.

It was planned that a poet would speak
to the winners, codicil to our thin conclusions.
The eyes downcast, he began reading
and his voice grew resonant:

'The night of the owl turned to defeated cumulus
and stagnant ponds of ancestral duty,
yes, and malignant waters.
It is necessary to swim under a reef
to reach the secret cave—
the locus of clamour and claw—
through evanescent waters
to the world of pure white clouds.'

Flying High

He held contest with the vegetable universe
that marks us at birth with its vigour.
'So, Princess, you know,' he said curtly
and jumped clear, leaving the others to the darkness.
'Okay, go ahead, towards the machine-guns.'
Quantities of time he had, and a pistol at his side,
holstered. A rush of disturbed swallows lifted up.
I have peered over his face: what art there is
in not mistaking his kneeling on water
or falling into the abattoirs.

The metallic birds swear by their prey.
The machine was a sword to hew a passage
to the future. If he could set fire to the water . . .
The aircraft guns roared, a signal,
and the winds bothered our ears.

Apparently the 'feel' of the surface of the fiord
was all wrong, and a vague mistrust followed the affair.
He stumbled often, but no one minded,
and then, hooking him back into his original pose
of quiet reflection, a peculiar smile
crept over his face, and he could not but obey.
Now he taunts the water, and then did my voice
build the coloured deceit in the vision:
I shall make it impossible for this swastika,
painted and venomous, to pierce the prairie.

That is what was so complicated: Schaffer appeared,
puffing, I knew what he was wet with,
dazed by the naked and ribald interventions:
he climbed up like a bird into a storm
of hostile aircraft but his friends were
still a hundred feet away. His lingo
was appropriate only to a German.

The end came suddenly, in English.
The airmen dispersed in the fog of luck,
a *whoof-whoof-whoof* of angels' light.
The rest of me flopped back into the very desire
that was always beyond him.

Pussy Willow

Yes, he did do wrong, this harum-scarum
boy who had got a wilful fit on him,
and a nature apt to tantalise.
He can make suggestions so sly and then
apologise with pink cakes and lemonade,
and hope to be forgiven—for what?

Mother went upstairs in a convulsion
as prim as a colt in a shuddering embrace,
singing blithely as she entered the room
kept locked for generations. She,
an obediently ascending bird
looked pale with relief. 'So I am in love.'

SOUND EFFECTS: Knock, knock . . . When
grandfather, in his too rigid state,
awash with catalogs, pounded the floor again,
his bearded rage astonished the century.
What now for the hymns of lust that flow
between the old gentleman and his charge?

'Begin our little play! It is nightfall—
in this measley tale, the woman settles down
to appraise the new men,' cried Meg.
'I don't want any new ones,' muttered Jo.
'I assert my work of novel glory in the tongs.
My wishes are my mausoleum, and my doom.'

Thus she of the wavy locks wailed petulantly,
and stood aloof, though she quaked a little
at the hero's rude touch. 'It isn't the things
on the sound track that bother me. It's the hidden
goings-on. You have lived out of bounds. No,
don't wink and grimace; winking is wrong.'

'While you're sneering at least you could
atone for the fun at the sunny window,' cried Meg,
who knew a good time when she saw one.
'How the vile emotional morass messes up
the voting patterns, and vexes the social process.'
MYSELF: 'So long, if you won't let me help you,

or shake you! I go to tell our fairy decorator
there are no more little people to be so adorned.
Lollipops and leprechauns, consumer durables,
your brain is drummed and flattened with this stuff.
The old President warned us in his wisdom
that a comfortable universe cripples us at birth.'

'Oh fudge,' retorted Meg, whose gloves,
like pair of dancing moths, spoke to the deaf:
to wit, the limping handyman, an injured guy
who, at a midnight tête-à-tête an age ago,
had held her sister in a crude embrace.
Everything went watery, decades passed:

she was dismayed to find that on the rebound
she had married a Major, done a tour of duty
in some flyblown army depot in the desert,
then washed up in a suburb thronged with wives.
Military life surprised her with its deft routines,
and gave each act a sense of political aptness.

One evening, wits akimbo, lost in the mirror
in silvery garb, Meg found herself
at peace, suddenly content, even euphoric.
OLD MAN: 'We shall all rest snug tonight.'
His augury began to unravel its sly
portentous meaning, and the play began.

Smaller Women

I resigned to tell mother a secret sign,
insolent napkin. But it's natural to commit a crime,
the second dose of germs that make you cross,
and then the moral lapses teach us
    with their beaks.

Among the crimes you botched, were you not
floating up to heaven in a frock? 'Bless you,
bless the solemn symphony of duty.'
Grudging duty, that is, to quickly quell
    a pallid polka

or pump up a yelping shiver to a spasm,
the kind that young gentleman only hear about
rattling their rusty skates among the rafters.
I came here young, able and long-shanked
    and left limping.

Oh, tell it to the horse marines, that if we were
agreeable, why, we were also—just a little—
ashamed of our pink hissy fits. Thus taught,
'Shiftless, have done for, knock and enter.'
    So, knock it off.

As the slumbrous subject of heaven glares
down on us, do the children aspire to a better
pedagogy? Bless your more sensitive arm.
And I may advertise—forgive me—
    a scribbled graph

that would paper over the filthy morass
to which you now offer amorous admission,
lures of tissue-paper, to clog the pale
epochs yawning on the baroque porch,
    your careless greed.

Transatlantic

Paris was not a place, it was the event,
and in that event the great writer
wrote about her grand obsession: herself.
Remember that the great writer liked
the evening telephone. The fade of age.

She said: snob strongly and snob often,
that was what she wanted.
If you go to the reading-rooms
as a result of smoking the herb of contempt
nothing you read will do you any good.
Why am I talking to you?

We received at least the evening sky
which was hers to inherit; that,
and a few thousand dollars.

My friendships after all, Helene said,
were based on direct emotion.
She did not stifle the great writer,
rather the work of the great writer
stifled others, a known council of vulgarisers.
You are journalists, Helene said,
you are all mechanical men.
Helene would be more inclined to violence, and
these femmes de menage stumbled into
a life filled with permanent anger.
Naturally it is a big explosion,
she yelled. You remember emotions.

The great writer had a mystic in to teach us
mysticism. He was attracted by Janet;
drop dead, Janet said. So he taught
moral tales, how ambition clogs the career.
Discretion is a kid of dilution, courtesy a limp.

O far shore, wrote the voice.

They met in the Luxembourg Gardens and
paperback in hand, turned to rend
what was left of my love story—
dark intellectual comments,
later printed in those Moral Tales.

There were traces in the enormous room
of what had made them.
Just stay here. We spent hours there.
To have lain with a little book.

Oh, drink, bring peace to the flesh.

Under Tuscan Skies

In the calm of a Lyons' Tea Shop near Piccadilly
punctuated with rustling noises and clinkings,
Edward found himself looking back
on his time in Tuscany. He had seen it then
as 'the life so short, the craft so long to learn',
in fact venomous to endure, those
horrible neighbours, but useful fodder
for his writing project, at the time, but now
in the British gloom it seemed fleeting and fruitless,
like the life of a white foam flake
amid a clashing of steel knives and hot looks—
why had he written it up in the form of little
poems, clotted with factitious insights?—
tissue-paper in a threshing machine—in fact,
he now prefers the incomplete circle of his drafts
to the blunt certainty of the finished book, as
the months of hope spent plotting his holiday
were better than the awful actuality.
What had he written? Watery flashback—

The ancient Roman sun preserves the sky,
reserving his warmth to faithfulness,
shining upon the undismayed towers,
whose images enscrolled the situation.
Lucy, recently rebuffed, sat speaking her mind
to her frequent and attentive male companion,
to hew a passage to his understanding.
'He, the God of Love and Shopping
may not have been hurt by your bruising snub,
to Him it's just water off a cold shoulder,'
she murmured, nudging closer. Would
clutch come to seize? And seize
to feed a passion? Eager boys, she knew,
would be prostrate at her feet, if they could.

A conversation in the forest, the grove
that borders the municipal zoo:
Her sex makes a brief longing.
—Thank you, more of the same.
I went straight to the heart of the matter.
—My dear, gentlemen are different.
But these two ladies are as bright as possible.
—Then what are you made of?
The same stuff as parsons are, but
with a warmer blood in my body.

They were walking about like restless animals,
ursine, almost blasphemous in their excessive exercise.

In a deft aside Edward explained the meaning
of the landscape, I mean the Mediterranean.
It was satisfying to imagine those huge
geological forces striving for a million years
to provide a vista that perfectly illustrated
certain Romantic imaginings that gushed out of
the tail-pipe of the Industrial Revolution.

The scene: The arrival. *The action:* She knew.
Lucy rehearsed her emotions under Parnassus,
till the late hour caught in her throat.
I was young fool! That fight with the driver!
Blunder, irretrievable, and so forth.
The clumsy dolt. Social gaffe. Red face.
Lucy, wincing, understanding everything.
Ow! He will never forgive me! Fuck it!

But why should she be upset? She's just a girl,
and one day as a lady she will sweep away
the wraiths that cloud the view, just as
a Viennese mind doctor with a gesture
calms a dog. Now, at muggy midnight,
she found herself alone on the road,
engraving her love malignantly upon a stone,
as a seething of hyacinths breathed
upon the hushed evening. So be it!
In the snows of recognition there is little warmth
and less life; better to guess and hesitate.
Now a storm yells and clambers over the horizon,
battering rain herds them into a shelter,
among the shadows comes forgiveness,
a prison of green centuries gladly huddled into.
Shuddering they reach out for
one another's mortifying spasms . . .

I had read, Edward murmured to himself,
that the floods of love in their urgent spate
magnify a horoscope, and that the god of fate,
leaning on the sky, counts our chances
on enormous fingers—so let the storm cease:
now the world is soaked and glittering,
and the young lovers creep back to find
their place in it, among the clattering traffic
and the rattle of cups.

Year Dot

I read of how one hushed
peasant, his aphorisms
of the loaded zodiac cursing
the street, desires a double garage.

A little pamphlet remains,
printed on a skull; new
images of genteel property
lean over the coloured board:

icons of fur and coffee,
the solemn symphony of a tree,
the silver nymph dozing
in a sleek modern kitchen.

Waking, her rage and enchantment
tremble in the language, her
beast's mouth and lashing tail.
The nymph from her elegant home

offers furious love
under an entertaining sky.
The striped fish move
through a new architecture.

Nightfall, and I must sleep in this
quaint shack, shades drawn,
inscribing the heart's stuttering
graph upon a dark glass,

nodding where the cockroach
applauds at his own funeral.
Now, a plausible future: in a
family home with ample furniture

I shall live as an imprisoned ghost.
Slow riot, enough sleep. Fate in my left
pocket, purple sky above: the rear lane
access allows my adieu. *Adieu!*

The Urn of Loneliness

Morton opened the diary: 'The hot flush of Angela's lips
tasted of her dual nature, when she kissed me . . . '
Mary was mooning over her, but this loose dance

had awakened a desire for a sterile kiss—
now starting to kiss her, meeting
in the physical pain, the focus of a strong drug

and her voice not giving out its meaning
for Angela, for the men crowded at the bar,
those whom 'Lesley' adored, her fierce look

gathering in chairs, pictures,
the metal birds looking on, their
mocking chided her, and would distract her,

so she shook her head—she felt
bruised, bitterly helpless. And 'Lesley'—
she found herself staring at 'Lesley'!

She had an ugly red scar down the skull
and a wart on her dark lids, those eyes
that would gaze with repugnance on Mary.

Was 'Lesley' loving Mary, or placidly grazing?
'Lesley' was no more the restrained person.
She must stop kissing this little marred face . . .

Her voice had brought the jungle—lions
are their emotions. 'Yes, those emotions.
They were not divine that night,' said Morton.

They had lived in their green descant of love
for months, but now, sainted with contempt,
Mary must lift her attentions to that purpose

of a dark eclipse, failing in spite of her cunning
to detect the chains of an ancient duty.
Because she was so like a beast, she felt,

she had put out her hand to 'Lesley'
who was still forgiving an endless cruelty.
Mary would clutch her coat, moist yet tawdry,

timid yet dissident. She recoiled at Morton's touch.
She looked over these sunken sodden wretches,
saying 'The terror, why can't they understand?'—

'Lesley' rushed in to talk to her once more
in the long night, these were torments to Morton.
'Is it my fault,' he cried, 'that the sad autumn of Mary

turned into hate? That Mary's anger
gave way to shame?' 'Don't look,'
Mary stammered. She knew she had a shame,

called 'normal'. Why had she let 'Lesley' mutter
'I want to arrive at the so-called normal,'
and not curtail that gaffe? Morton closed the book.

New Poems: Europe

At the Tomb of Napoleon

They handed me the French Army on a plate,
half a million fresh young bodies. I made
a meal of it, and came back for more.

Now six nested coffins and a ton of marble
shield me from the grief of those old people
who fed their children to the Cannibal God.

Bats

In a freezing attic somewhere in Prague
a hungry songwriter invents Sincerity, but alas,
too early. A decade later, a popular singer,
struck by the intimacy a microphone fakes,
invents a way of sobbing in time to the music—
earnest little hearts are wrecked
from San José to Surbiton. The angelic
choirs, should they be tempted to rebel,

would they hit on a trick so lucrative? Clouds
of butterflies reassure us: we are so much more
serious, and intelligent—think of rockets, and
the invention of dentistry and napalm. Sincerity?
It will take a Poet Laureate to turn it to profitable use.
Bats circle the Old City, low and silent.

Care and Feeding of a Small Poem

Allow enough sunlight. Ignore
that traffic, it's going nowhere.
Wear something nice. When I smile,

smile. Write an entry in your diary
that will display, to future generations
of grieving fans, your fastidious manners.

Don't let on how you grovelled
and sobbed when you were ten.
Stay away from violent or distressing movies.

A special recipe would go well here:
the baked eel you fondly imagine
everyone likes. And a watercolour,

or, failing the talent for that, a photograph
of a child on an empty, rain-soaked beach.
Write about how you live life to the full,

despite the migraine and the panic attacks.
Now secure all this in a locked box
and throw away the key.

Manikin de Vin

They're all lined up under the lights,
Christmas tinsel stuffing their mouths.
And now a cloud hides behind that hill,
arguing about philosophy. In the distance,
a murmur, perhaps below ground: yes,
it comes from the tunnels filling up
with commuters commuting, no one knows why
on this day given to festivities.
The French, they say, have a word for it,
something to do with eating in the open air,
and now they spit the tinsel out. Hesitating,

I had meant to write, he wrote—too late,
the intended recipient has dropped off the twig
into the South Pacific, still he writes on:
The days seem endless here . . . lucky fellow,
his future written out on the little label
on the back of a bottle of claret: you will live
forever, says the manikin in the sketch,
but none of your wishes will ever come true.

On a Noted Vista

This high view
speaks to itself, like a Contents Page
in a closed book left in a room
and forgotten for generations.
The weak sunlight passes across
the window, day by day.

So, the view, such as it is: a beach
queried by waves, repeatedly;
a trace of cloud high up, busy
with its patient, lazy exploration
of that empty blue field.

Alas, no explications
are expected.

Grief, in small allotments.

A shame to camp here
under empty Heaven
with nothing much to do,
notes the petulant bird
called to the motley colours
of his old, old clan.

And of course a flower—
precious, on this field of snow
or blinding coral sand—has its
back turned on us, and its face
to the cosmos, the grand intricate machine
that brought it into being
through a chain of devourings
thoroughly understood by all.

A Poet in the Reading Room

A boardroom coup: a dozen angels gather
to make up a quorum. They quarrel, then agree:
a duly constituted realm of clouds would rather
something fluent in D-moll. Must they see
housewives in fur coats parade Fifth Avenue,
and endure flattened fifths in a suburban train?
The Master has a headache; his cherubs know
no remedy but art birching the brain.

The Kappelmeister cautiously declines to dance.
Is this the destiny of counterpoint? Elsewhere
a golden boy squanders an inheritance
in a vain attempt to fudge up a career.
The Old Man's investing in the 'lighter-than-air':
a hundred-dollar bill ignites his cigar.

Stage Door

The nymph Syrinx
takes a drag on a cigarette.
She's waiting outside the stage door
for the lesbian country-and-western singer
impersonator. No one's going to
turn her into a pan-pipe, she thinks.

A police car cruises past. The passenger
is talking to someone on the police radio—
'No, not the crossword, the *cryptic* crossword.
You just have to look at the thing, for Chrissake!
Hey, Charlie, that was a red light.'

It's growing dark—a curtain of rain
is moving down from the mountain range
behind the town, and soon the lights
will be reflected in a sheet of water
streaming over Main Street.

Thistles

'. . . *Working on Modernism*
while the stark grey thistles push to the door.'
—Peter Porter, 'Affair of the Heart'

A chill mist rises from the ground to meet
dusk descending over pigeon-spattered monuments.
Somewhere in this over-crowded grey metropolis
a poet puts away his notes on blooms and horticulture
and turns to his day job, copy-editing
'Fodder Plants for British Herbivores'. The author
keeps misspelling 'ungulates'. From the radio,
a meteorologist addresses the weather—

winter dragging its wet hem across Wales—
then offers a bouzouki whining to itself.
In the little kitchen smelling of fresh paint
a kettle starts to shriek its head off.
The poet works on 'Thistles', while
Modernism pushes at the door.

Whisper

Close by the bones of Joshua Blane
paving is laid, and tiles are hoisted up,
ochre and grey-green, and wedged between slats
in thick stacks. High up, dirty dishwater cloud
botches heaven again, tends to apricot and ash-black
as it should, must—now while the wicked clock
is thinking, diesel quarrels with diesel, executives
ponder the employment of cabling
and its guest electrons. Flavour is an abstraction,
even if you can feel it—behind the glass of wine
a manufacturing sector switches on
and the motors begin their old complaint.

Now the dazzle falls from the sky
at purple dusk, glitter sprinkling down
on the lucky citizens of Oligopolis
and on the lawn a drawling colonial accent
fondles and enriches every idle comment
turning shopping into a kind of predestination.

The folding table folds up and rolls away
and a First Aid kit has lots to tell us:
traffic, old musicians, polystyrene—
we all have a right to speak, and an obligation
to pay attention to the slightest whisper.

New Poems: Speech to Text

Anguish

The May frostbite is still on the land,
a statement by analogy
down by John Quinn.
We should assess this.
Single men sit through the night.
Force a dual key to a bloody game
on the issue in this exhibit
to see more of the sea.

Flying, all share a common fear.
Get a file, he said, she's
come here with this shot deal, no pay
and no exit. Kinda nice to know that,
thanks for joining in the song
at the close, four years.

Bottom of the Harbour

Maria today got a heap of stuff,
all she can use for a month.
Taylor said she should make one
for the Indian, that is, the male person
originally from the subcontinent
and since she just wasn't being the buyer
for two of them, she said no.
This had an effect on the warrior courtroom

until all of that month had gone by,
or do you mean that the US should give up
the Cold War tactics shown on the
Canton blankets? We use them to keep warm,
for goodness' sake, it's a case of being up at dawn
bottom-feeding in and around the drowned cathedral.

Deluge

Upgrading the late edition for all US units.
So why didn't you move the stock?
That one guy got a new all-nuclear crisis
for the week of the invasion of twenty people—
Congress and the effect of the debates.
Find a buyer who is in the American party.
I mean you'll visit downtown Los Angeles.
You do not get that on the internet.

That busy team has no qualms about going on and on,
the later we delivered the women to encourage the men
to get that problem solved—it became a key
that unlocked the pain of the Soviet Union,
and today a new location for the quiz shoot,
a green meadow filled with buttercups.

Departure

As a view
of the busy sale
quantity sat on a DVD
and this one
is also your mistake
when you
listen to the ABC
on the pound and the dollar

or the euro
on a fix—
so much for
the public
who know it
in the wallet.

Horticulture

Thomas Cecil, what did you do?
A man can he get what he wants
on the inside—much good did that do me.
Thomas was sued by the city
because he gave a false statement
when he came to the desert resort
which was not open, to peel an idea.
That means they'll not nominate—that is—

because of the delay they called to say
that the sea—no, the Warsaw pact countries
mainly lack seas, thus navies, whose diet can never
be shown because of the jelly bean component.
If Greece gives someone a permanent visa status
it means that the Jewish faith cannot do for old Thomas.

Lives

Put me on the list of local media maniacs.
I am an old man working on a dBase file,
and I know that all the men in the theater
are there for a reason. It's my fault
that date got to be bearish. I knew a student
with a hearing aid, and then the insane visual
was invented, the Enola come-on. Come on,
I can't hear you. Take the kids to see the conditions
caused by the Vietnam War, why don't you?

They're not humane in Dawson City.
It seems to me that your famous design champion
is up a tree, and what effect does that have
on the practical Mister? Mama must do
what she must, shut down by the videotape marshal
as a mandate for the people of Mormon.

Marinara

Michelle speaks especially to Cleveland:
'the CIA did sit in, that is, sit in
their offices on this issue also—
they come on down the steps
outside the Capitol, chanting initials:
NATO the FBI most US troops—blah
blah—then it's denial and denial.'
Marina, this should be a speech from a script

worked up in the story conference room
of your dreaming self: Don't hide it,
your life will be on film: the entire avalanche, the whole
disaster, the cascades of shit and honey, someday
tilting in the sky over England like a Dornier—
a blast crucial one single family and now gone.

Metro

Two guys from Detroit pored over the suicide letter
as its auction price rose through the $8.00 range.
A male choir that this year sang in Vietnam
is now a medical team on a training course.
No one wants an incontinent hostage.
Femina's call for us all to share the pretty things
fell on deaf ears; so much for the taste of justice.
They can't be bought. An application in the name of Antonov

will not reveal me as a donor or a smaller companion.
We could use a dime when the music imitates a disaster area.
The idea is still to issue a new Long Beach five-point
major disaster this year. At the home they can vote
that the economy is in fact the city of events
and he says 'no one is a real actor in the film.'

Movements

The Gulf of Aden did enough, but
you know I said to kill one of those bad
men on Friday, bring the body to me later.
To call the team 'failures' would make this
a political stumble. If someone on Dataquest's young
and wants to get a CD in a bid to secede why
in the affidavit of being—why did you—
like all the kids in the city why should they—

but I do not cause the economy.
Is that what the song says? If you go from the beach to
the hotel for the Young and the Stupid, you'll get
the idea that we don't need more trees, just more
people who sit on the dish, this sounds fine and energetic
so they should be going out on a shaman basic poster.

Parade

The dollar goes to a city that is his only speaking song
that took place in the open air
and we also collected data based on a list
of all the costs of Saint Keene,
it's a CD of fall songs, maybe, only
the data is in a format that might give away
the occupation of the person, and
as we got onto the shuttle, a flashlight shone on the ticket.

So the district judge knows that I am still at large.
That was the goal of the donors the courts imprisoned.
They added a goal to motivate the contestants
and that's among the ideas they need to speed up:
the one who negotiates with NATO will always be
sad: the ideas of all the songs have always been known.

Pronto

1

No joy in this one, Bob. Would you like to be
summoned for one little blot on the record,
by a marshal? And create the indictment
today, that will be used for a demo
tomorrow? If you do that, my old friend,
the problem seems to be saying, the data
will go on the skids—it could be a fun contest
held in a field in the Boston area.

Now I don't want you to get the idea that
finding a guitar has anything to do with it.
Just dish it up like the boss wants: though
if you deal with the CIA—Hi—I'm Bob.
Can't talk now. Down in the park,
listening to the guitars, lots of single mothers . . .

2

Do they need to show more, to agree to put
the data mining double digits to use?
They blame a hotel trustee ten to one.
A bang on the gong and he's off to Brooklyn
with a call for a song set from Tony, sliding to CNN,
sun blinding him, trouble in the upper airway,
cost of sales data ballooning—he cannot operate.
It is the 'FM in a Domain Name System' hazard,

a haphazard collapse they can share with the boss
who already believes that we should solve it—
that must be what the publishers want—
two weeks' extra pay, he would say that to keep me,
but I'm getting used to his lies. Sufficient unto the day
are its many small evils—Betty, comment on that, pronto.

Royalties

We'll make common cause with the Right,
and take that message to the Ford Foundation
who helped the CIA guy in Paris win a medal
that let him sit in on the cultural deliberations
of all those old freaks. Also note
that the quote of the week missed me altogether,
that is, I missed it—I just stopped by
to look in on the literary debate, cast a vote . . .

Democracy is what we define it to be.
Sure the Iranians voted in a government,
but those socialist shits were going to nationalise—
their oil, British oil, our oil, what the hell—
so we put in that poet guy to agitate, Bunting.
Sure, people were killed: so what?

Scenes

The subcommittee poses a threat.
When they say 'the DB city' they don't mean
the Deutsche Bahn AG or whatever . . . here
the board of trade shows what to import, the—
Ronald, get them! Don't shout! or give orders.
We told the customer what the customer wants.
We've only potted palms, and one wolf a year.
Then all the comedians disembark in San Diego.

That's a company with a real future, though
the double stop is daunting, I agreed with them,
and I should say that the fondled sale failed
on the killed day, a reminder about the order for Tivoli
this week, they even want to set up in the courtroom.
We'll all need visas, and openness cannot be fear.

Shames

Don't kid me, I'm not Noah.
The corps existed in the new data—
Esprit de Corps, I mean—I mean giveaway,
no way—people see the wheel
then get a phenomenal fright.
No one thought he did it—she and the Nazi salt,
baking bread in a cosy home in the Midwest.
That was a duplicate of a shopping mall.

Call me 'wish of the mall' and no,
I don't want the Tutsi player.
Make a decision on the whole movie:
good or bad. Mary is no relation.
Kitty cat, you force the Nazi salute.
I need what? A system of stone?

Sorehead

I was arrested because of that internal memo,
and ended up in a cell, then I was told
to sit with the police and the main
state and local bigwigs.
If you need a portal, reduce the safety margin
on the airport risk factor, they said, and I got the blame.
An unaltered, PA six-pack call at 6 cents a day
minus expenses, and see who belongs.

The local cop would not open the tomb of the deported—
sorry, departed—as usual he wanted to tell me a story.
The goal is a pool of all new CC research, he said:
they need a set of three standard deviations.
A TV ad face makes comments, what would they know.
Open the tomb, and let me in.

Story

The Seagate exited at the same time, telling him
to make a profit, but he found only enough
to get by. They're holding a playboy, he is still on the sofa,
unconscious. Fit the company's last item
in a dizzying array, then consider the eulogy
you posted on the internet, you with your bail mind-set,
no one was even in jail at that time, not holding
in the closet the nation, the nation a house.

Today a new philosophy: and they testified
to shut down certain data pathways, not wanting
the bullet, the use of an application, so-called.
The big guy looks just like you, the DNA test
gets the nod. In the scene that you may not know,
the surgeon is on CNN and then it goes dark.

Subcontinent Nocturne

Units of troops learn to fear what the body seeks.
People don't care what the law allows you to display:
a city full of media, before we're torn to pieces
in the Class A data stack. And who used to be
happy in a dungeon, pray tell, tied up with the
Swedish maid? Don't believe all the FAA tells you.
The radio waves to the north of Bombay tell
the young programmers to want to win, to be on a cool team,

to demand a training lesson that gets them into the call centres
full of money. Player after player falls,
a large old domain is sold to the man in a blue suit.
But the town seems a bit tedious on the trip back
from the airport—after California, it's a dump—
I hear the city's soulful call—don't leave me again.

Villas

1

In April, the sun was to be the display manager.
What I am will eat it, data about the team.
Maybe it's just good enough to keep doing that
since the ideas expressed fake up the stock and bond count.
He can want to win a token of the Norwegian fake,
he wants to believe that this can be a diminished fifth
and so what's the issue—Las Colinas:
is it that the girl's address?

or should it be that the pocket books, on the night,
open to a page where the Sonics become better known
as teammates on a vital mission to the azure quandary.
I've been booked in the media mall citadel—
data flows and then the syndrome.
No, I do not want to address the Iraqis.

2

The video shows that they can all be
what they want to be, until the Cleveland full moon
strikes, and they get a quick one on the side, and
they both wanted an eighteen-city police commissioner
to call us on the new board. The quality is suitable
for that, though I should point out that
a check for Washington today doesn't mean promotion,
so I don't suppose the Vatican regards pride

as the product that would determine
the station's campaign of violence—okay,
call me—it only costs a dime—in time to
shut down the TV show. Go on, say some more.
You post the key to a college guy here, I get off,
the companion you can't see, who sees everything.

New Poems: At the Movies

Shadow of a Doubt

Handsome Uncle Charlie, burdened by crime.
He laughs and scatters gifts, but he looks
unwell—no, he's fine—the man playing cards
looks sick—he has a full hand of spades,
but then, he gets to tell the story about
how the ace of spades leads the pack.
Suspicion follows you like a snake in the grass,
so the story is torn up. But destroying the evidence
points to the evidence. Sleeping dogs lie.
Now, should a girl tell on the bad man?
It would kill Mother. But Uncle Charlie
has been killing plenty of those, it seems,
the fat, lazy, greedy widows eating cake
and wasting money—they deserve to die.
Now those two men are here to see you,
again—something about a survey,
counting all the happy American families
and listening closely to their apple-pie opinions
as they look down from a high window through
shade-dappled branches at a pair of neighbours
pausing for a gossip in the sun. On the busy street
the old traffic cop can't help the girl, he's
avuncular and normal, and he has a job to do.
Now everything falls to pieces
and a killer pleads for his life. Traffic
everywhere, an engine running and leaking gas,
then back on the train again, the train
that takes you out into the horrible world.
The man with all the cards is here, somewhere,
behind the viewfinder, watching everything,
a resident alien with a point of view.
Uncle Charlie has to die, we all knew that,
it just took a while to fall into place
in front of a speeding black locomotive
somewhere out of town, and far away.

North by Northwest

A hero breasts Manhattan traffic, always
ready to stop off at a tourist destination.
A blunder with a telegram and Mother—
a demon never seen, only hinted at
in her distant, comfortable castle—
will lose her little boy, who quickly
plunges into an irritating adventure
in the picaresque mode—leaping
to conclusions as the scenery reels past,
into bed and out again, dodging and weaving
across a landscape more deadly and bucolic
with each passing trick of the light.
Of course it's post-postmodern to have the hero
an advertising man rather than a policeman-detective
tough-guy action type, and the crop-dusting plane scene
is funny and priceless. Perhaps the Master was trying to
lighten up after Vertigo. There's no fun there, just
descending levels of madness and sadness.
The blonde, unlike his sainted Mother,
is very good and also devious and wicked,
and so roller coaster morals are the norm
and in fact this unravelling storm of incidents
and grief is the painful future due to us
when we stumble blinking into the light,
for this sequence of parables was built
by its huge crew of many talents to be seen
and heard in the crowded dark, the wicked
are found out and trampled on, another
train, another bed, good night.

Dark Passage

Poor Vincent Parry: he rolls out of a garbage can
and stumbles through a valley of coincidences,
falling into the lap of a blonde.

Poor Vincent: we are locked inside his head,
seeing everything, feeling nothing but vertigo
as the screen swoops and wobbles with his weaving
and ducking to avoid his fate. He can't
have a drink, we would get splashed,
he dare not look in a mirror, because
we would be there gawking, dismayed . . .

Poor Vincent: he gets disfigured by a man with a towel
and a razor, and wakes up tied to the bed.
Madge calls, and whispers, and goes away,
and calls back again, spying, sneaking a drink, and
every fragment of conversation ends with Madge
who, if she can't have what she wants,
kills it. Vincent gets punched around
and a pal gets it, beaten to death with a trumpet.
Madge, fatal Madge, fallen Madge,
defenestrated Madge on the sidewalk.

Ah, Vincent: he used to look handsome
with a pencil-thin moustache, then he woke up
looking like some movie star. He wants to
call out in his bad dream: Untie me!
Set me free! But he will not be free
until he takes the bus to distant Peru
alongside a boring couple of jerks
who have just stumbled over each other
in a bus station of all places.

Vincent dreams that he sits in a white jacket
sipping a drink by the moonlit beach in Peru,
feeling anxious until the music changes
and a blonde appears: Well, tie me down,
and start me dancing.

Girl in Water

(Vertigo)

Waiting to meet a pretty girl—any pretty girl—
hot summer day in 1958, beach crowd, emotional algebra,
also list and remember: makeup, perfume, lipstick, talc,
telephone passion—no, a soda fountain, a pizza.

Do they dream of mystery and adventure, women?
or do girls want to drown in literature? No, stupid. I
bet she'd like a fragrant pizza topped with mozzarella,
or is that just me? A movie: Item: Kim Novak. A drive-in—

yes, more subtle and powerful appetites litter the sand.
So become that detective, wounded, pitiful; so
learn to love and fail in love in the back row at the Bijou,
in parked cars, or snug among sandhills . . . your spyglass a nib,

keyhole secrets memorised and filed away, until
eternity comes calling at the foot of a staircase.
After that ending, another climb, another cliff
beyond which something awful awaits: love

or falling in love or into love or falling into death, a
uniform and dizzying and swift descent
that leaves you breathless, leaves you
very unsteady like a cork in the water,

effervescent and febrile and emotionally labile,
ready for almost anything.
That conscious pilot spoke: scripsi quod scripsi:
I have written what? I have written for

girl in water 'girl in water', girl
or woman in waves of water. I,
keen to find behind mirrors, wavering echoes, burn
in plots and complex narratives to draw

many clues out, threads of meaning. A
new insight into the convoluted plot
of good and evil I can look for, where good men whine,
villains struggle to prevail and bluster

against ordinary background noise and hubbub:
kaleidoscopes of criminality and subtle fiscal judo
scam and prosper, and some ordinary guy
will win and lose everything. I

owe more than money. The key will turn:
nervous ex-detectives afraid of causing harm
drop into floods of anxiety, plunge into semi-
enervating doubt; whirlpools of suspicion, and later

refuse help from well-meaning friends or
from glum old girl-friends, dawdling, doodling, who
understand too well their weaknesses, their
lack of manly self-respect, who know how hypnotic

those doubled mysteries within a mystery are. You reach
into a maelstrom of neurosis. Beyond bodily desire,
these complex chess-like fantasies are the true romantic
scenes in your life: the most ludic acrostic paradises: click!

Black and White

(*The Three Faces of Eve*)

Everything loose, including the morals:
first one, then the other, a kind of sister:
a headache, a beating, and the bad one sneaks out
and chokes the child. Or is the better self
just a sober lady dying to have some fun?
And look, no coloured folk: the streets
are full of white Americans taking a stroll.
At night there are crowds dancing and smoking,
which is also fun, or drinking alcohol,
that pool of mystery and regret.
She thinks: Put on the red dress.
Take it off. Say hello to the nice Doctor.
He frowns and looks concerned, and quickly
consults with an older, wiser man. Then he
writes it up, but we never see him
writing it up. He doodles with a pen at night.
Somewhere back in the fifties: the sound
of a typewriter clacking and a little bell
punctuating the script, I mean the story, that is,
the case notes. More fun in a red frock
in a truck, then nostalgia. Soon there are three women
arguing and hating each other, then
one of them starts forgiving one of the others.
First her sorrow and concern
for that other woman, then mine.
Where does she get the energy?
It's the headache, stupid. Try divorce,
and become a better human being, as if
that would help. Nothing keeps death at bay.
Somewhere a nicer person is moving
slowly towards me. When it's time to say goodbye
I'll die, just like that, for her sake. For my sake.
Say goodbye. Never leave me.

From *Selected Poems* 1982

The Popular Mysteries

A fact is as real as
you make it, and your complex
dreaming is a gift factory

as silly as a lucky dip, as
basic as a traffic accident.
And after a quick lunch on the Harbour,
a drink picks you up and you
drift off the surface of the planet
daft, adolescent and deeply wise:

a fine glow lights up
your lazy limbs and the nerves
drop away. Behind the blue horizon
a boat disappears, popular mysteries
begin. You hear voices. You're
asleep, and thoroughly happy.

Acknowledgments

I should like to thank my wife Lyn who has patiently supported my work for many decades; also the Australia Council Literature Board and the NSW Government Ministry for the Arts, who at various times have supplied invaluable support in terms of grants and fellowships, and the Cultural Relations Section of the Department of Foreign Affairs for assistance with reading tours of the US, Canada and Europe.

I'd also like to thank the Faculty of Arts and the Humanities Research Centre at the Australian National University; the School of Humanities and Social Science at the New South Wales Institute of Technology; the Department of English and Linguistics at Macquarie University; the International Programs Office of Rollins College at Winter Park, Florida; and the English Faculty, the Judith Wilson Bequest and Jesus College at Cambridge University for their hospitality and support during the times I spent with them as visiting scholar or writer-in-residence.

Finally, thanks are due to the editors of the publications in which these poems first appeared, sometimes in a different form: ABC Radio National, *Active, Reactive: Literary Arts Review, Adelaide Review, Age Monthly Review, The Age, Alliance Française* magazine, *Ambit* [UK], *Angel Exhaust* [UK], *Antipodes, Antithesis, Artforce, Atlanta Review, Australian Book Review, B City* [US], *The Best Australian Poetry* [2003, 2004, 2005], *Best Verse, Big Bridge* [Internet], Booksmith.com, *Boxkite, Brisbane Review, Bulletin, Canberra Times, Conjunctions, Conspire* [Internet], *Cordite: Poetry and Poetics Review, Cortland Review, Critical Quarterly* [UK], *East Village Web* [Internet] *Eureka Street, Eye Dialect, Fulcrum* [US], *Fusebox* [US], *Grand Street* [US], *Heat, Hermes, HOBO Poetry Magazine, Jacket, Journal of the Literature and Philosophy Society, Journal of the Sydney Personal Computer Users' Group, Kenyon Review, Kunapipi, Landfall* [NZ], *Leviathan* [UK], *London Review of Books, Makar, Meanjin, Nation Review, New American Writing, New Poetry,* OpenOffice.Org, *Otis Rush, Outrider: A Journal of Multicultural Literature in Australia, Overland, papertiger, Paris Review, Parnassus* [US], *Phoenix Review, Picador New Writing 3, Pitch* [UK], *Poetic Voices* [Internet], *Poetry* magazine [US], *Poetry Australia, Poetry International* [Internet], Poetry International London catalogue, *Poetry International* magazine [US], *Poetry Kit* [Internet], *Poetry Review* [UK], *Postmodern Culture* [Internet], *Quarterly Review of Literature Singapore* [Internet], Radio France Culture, *Salt, Scripsi, Shearsman* [UK], *Southerly, Surfers Paradise* [Sydney], *Sydney Morning Herald, Thylazine* [Internet], *Times Literary Supplement, Triquarterly* [US], *Ulitarra, Verse* [UK, US], *Voices, Web Del Sol* [Internet], *Weekend Australian Magazine, Weekend Australian, Westerly, Works on Paper* [Cambridge, UK].

Notes: at johntranter.com

Printed in the United States
134137LV00002B/119/A